THE

REAGAN DETOUR

Richard Reeves

SIMON AND SCHUSTER *New York*

Published by Simon and Schuster
A Division of Simon & Schuster, Inc.
Simon & Schuster Building
Rockefeller Center
1230 Avenue of the Americas
New York, New York 10020

SIMON AND SCHUSTER and colophon are registered
trademarks of Simon & Schuster, Inc.

Designed by Irving Perkins Associates
Manufactured in the United States of America

10 9 8 7 6 5 4 3 2 1
10 9 8 7 6 5 4 3 2 1 pbk.

Library of Congress Cataloging in Publication Data
Reeves, Richard.
    The Reagan detour.

    1. Reagan, Ronald.   2. United States—Politics and
government—1981-   . 3. Conservatism—United
States.
I. Title.
E876.R428   1985   973.927′092′4   85-14171
ISBN: 0-671-60652-2
        0-671-60702-2 pbk.

This book is for Ken Auletta.
And for Don Singleton, Tom Corcoran and
Dick Harpster.

CONTENTS

CHAPTER I
THE POLITICS OF IDEAS   9

CHAPTER II
THE CONSERVATIVE REVOLUTIONARY   15

CHAPTER III
THE IDEAS INDUSTRY   23

CHAPTER IV
HOW MR. REAGAN BECAME MR. PRESIDENT   33

CHAPTER V
THE DEMOCRATS' FORCED MARCH   40

CHAPTER VI
WHAT IS A DEMOCRAT?   49

CHAPTER VII
WHO THE REPUBLICANS ARE   63

CHAPTER VIII
FINDING THE MAINSTREAM   79

CHAPTER IX
THE POLITICS OF INDIVIDUALISM   93

CHAPTER X
NEW CONSENSUS, NEW DEBATES   108

INDEX   135

CHAPTER I

THE POLITICS
OF IDEAS

ON November 6, 1984, the people of the United States voted for President, casting 53,426,357 ballots for the Republican incumbent, Ronald Reagan, to 36,930,923 for the Democratic challenger, former Vice President Walter Mondale. During the campaign and afterward, there was a great deal of talk and commentary about image and communication and personality. But, after all, it seemed clear that if Mondale had said and represented what Reagan did, and Reagan had spoken for the ideas and tradition that Mondale represented, then Mondale, not Reagan, would have won on that Tuesday. In the end, that is what politics is about: ideas.

President Reagan proved during the 1984 campaign that he was, in the cliché of the day, "a great communicator." It sometimes seemed that his command of the skills of his old profession, acting, enabled him to do what actors are supposed to be able to do: persuade their audiences to suspend disbelief. But the real power of Reagan the communicator was not a trick of the trade. It was the simple fact that he held a set of simple beliefs and was able to express them in simple and direct language. He did not sound like a politician, which made him a great politician.

Perhaps he will also prove to be a great leader. Certainly he is an extraordinary one. He began his political career as the spokesman of the minority wing of a minority party that had just suffered one of the worst electoral defeats in American history. Within twenty years, twenty rather uncompromising years, he had led that party to electoral victory as overwhelming as the original loss. In the process, he came to speak for millions of Americans who had come to believe that their ideas and values no longer had any place in the land of the free and the home of the brave. He articulated a new kind of American populism.

It was a spectacular personal triumph, but that did not make it a triumph of personality. What came to be known as "Reaganism" was at least as much the triumph of conservative intellectuals who, in their own words, "retreated into the wilderness" after the devastating Republican defeat of 1964. Working alone and in groups financed by very dedicated and very rich conservative businessmen, those thinkers of the right created a business themselves, the "ideas industry." Their product was paper and talk, just words. But they were words that gradually affected the way many Americans thought about themselves and about their relationship to government.

"What the Republicans accomplished during the last fifteen years was a triumph of ideas, an intellectual victory," said one of the Democratic Party's more important young thinkers. "They shifted the burden of proof onto government."

With Reagan doing most of the talking, the conservatives tried to change the way their countrymen thought. If they were not quite able to do that, they did have significant success in changing the way people looked at things in the 1980s. Really changing American thinking, after all, has proved to be an almost impossible task over more than two hundred

10

years of American history. In the late 1830s, Alexis de Tocqueville wrote this in *Democracy in America:*

> I hear it said that it is in the nature and habit of democracies to be constantly changing their opinions and feelings. . . . But I saw nothing of the kind among the great democratic people that dwells upon the opposite shores of the Atlantic Ocean. What struck me in the United States was the difficulty of shaking the majority once an opinion is conceived of. . . . The public is engaged in infinitely varying the consequences of known principles rather than in seeking for new principles.

The French visitor was only one of the first to recognize the extent and dominance of a set of shared assumptions and values that later generations of scholars would call "the American Creed" or "the American Ideology." The politics of the great democracy has always been bounded by those shared assumptions, the things that for all practical (political) purposes define American thinking about America. Americans created themselves as the people who believed in: *individualism*—the idea that societies exist to allow individuals to pursue happiness; *freedom*—the right to make any choices that don't infringe on the freedom of others; *equality*—the equal chance for one and all to compete for wealth and power; *private property*—the right to own and use the land and possessions each person can afford to buy; *democracy*—the idea that the only legitimate form of government is one in which each citizen shares in the power of public decision-making; *rule of law*—the principle that the power of officials and governments must be limited and restrained by written law, most particularly the Constitution of the United States.

Shared agreement around those fundamental principles made the United States among the most stable of countries and American politics among the most narrow. Americans agree on most things, certainly most big things. A debate between Americans of the Right and the Left on the basics of organizing a society—say between Ronald Reagan and Sena-

11

tor Edward Kennedy—would be pretty boring stuff to foreign politicians used to fundamental ideological clashes in day-to-day politics.

The American debate is about definitions and implementation; the debaters massage the symbols, polish them to try to catch public attention and even get people to see them a bit differently. By the 1980s, conservative thinkers had massaged them pretty well and Reagan did some nice polishing. The conservative President hit the old themes from a different direction and persuaded millions of others to take another look at government's role at home and America's stance in the world. They did, but that didn't always mean they liked everything they saw—or even everything they voted for.

If there was a pattern to the Reagan years it was that the President proposed and the public disposed. There was a constant and vigorous tug-of-war as Reagan, a very direct man for a politician, tried to do what he had said he would do and found himself pulling against a majority of the people who had just voted for or cheered for him. The President declared "Mandate!" again and again, and charged into a wall of consensus, again and again. Like popular presidents before him, he was regularly reminded that people had elected him on their terms.

President Reagan was able to change the American agenda in his time—what people looked at—but he was unable to change very much about America. In many ways, particularly in attacks on the concept of the welfare state, Reaganism was a failure from the beginning. Ronald Reagan, it seemed, thought he had been chosen in the name of self-reliance (and Christian charity) to dismantle the complicated apparatus of social welfare that had been built up over fifty liberal years that began with the election of Franklin D. Roosevelt as President in 1932. But he found out that he was only the guy who had been hired to rationalize the thing. A majority of Americans had concluded that something was wobbling out of control in Washington, but a greater majority shared beliefs in the concepts of protective government, government *for* the people. Reagan proved to be a principled and determined leader who won many battles, but lost his war to change the American direction. The Reagan years would be a detour, necessary if sometimes nasty, in the long progression of American liberal democracy. Americans seemed destined to choose political and social individualism over economic individualism, continuing to uphold and defend government, sometimes grudgingly, as the most trustworthy available protector against accumulations of wealth and the other sources and manifestations of private power.

If that government had become bloated and tyrannical, as Reagan had come to believe (after he had accumulated private position himself), he had earned the right to put it back in its place. He was right in much of what he said, according to most of the people in 1980 and 1984, and he did many of the things he said he would do. But as the great goals of the Reagan mission blended or faded back into the enduring realities of the American consensus, the arrogance of mission continued to shine brighter—particularly after November 6, 1984. There was a stink of arrogance rising in the heady air of Washington. The people in power were beginning to believe what they said about the reelected President and about themselves: that they spoke for all the people, that they spoke for America, that America was not only good but was right! Trouble could not be far away when the President, in a joke five months after his reelection, said that he had found an answer to the related problems of declining agricultural exports and bankrupted farmers: "I think we should keep the grain and export the farmers." Perhaps there would be a small war to topple an inconvenient government. Perhaps Federal budget deficits or trade balances would grow so big that they would topple, crashing into the national economy and the individual security of Americans. Perhaps there would be nothing more exciting than the scandal that usually followed small men into big places.

The Republicans had retained power in 1984 by projecting themselves as "America's Party," the party of patriotism and old-fashioned American values and pride. They were the party

13

of assimilation: the old Yankees and Protestants saying, "Be like us. Be real Americans." They were the guardians of "Americanism," the notion that "we know what's good in America and we know what's good for America." But that conceit has always had a way of becoming "We'll tell you what's good for you." If that happened, the Democrats would be back in power as fast as you could say "Nineteen eighty-eight."

Here, the people govern. Not parties or ideologies. Fast technology and quick Americans have produced a politics of individualism that quickly gives and quickly takes away power from the men and women who shape and understand ideas whose moment has come. So the last part of this book is about the ideas and issues that I believe will inevitably bring liberalism and the Democrats back into fashion and power—sooner rather than later.

The Democrats, I think, might focus on three areas: a redefining of "national interest" as the keystone of a modern foreign policy more sophisticated than an endless series of threats and commitments in every corner of the world and the heavens; a persuasive reaffirming of the best of the traditions of American populism, even a little bit of class warfare in some of the more exclusive corners of the country; and some creative pioneering on a coming range of issues concerned with the relationship between the work of each American and the productivity of the nation.

The point here is that elections and, ultimately, the direction of the country depend on ideas. American conservatives took control of the government of the country because they took that as the lesson of an election more than twenty years ago when their movement and their party, the Republican Party, seemed to have been destroyed in a confrontation between a not very nice man named Lyndon Johnson and a personable fellow named Barry Goldwater. Americans voted for and against ideas in 1964, and they did the same thing in 1984.

CHAPTER II

THE CONSERVATIVE REVOLUTIONARY

"IN this present crisis, government is not the solution to our problem," Ronald Reagan said two minutes into his Inaugural Address as President of the United States on January 20, 1981. "Government is the problem."

A consistent man, at least rhetorically. He attacked the government even as he took it over, as he had been attacking it since the day he had become a national political figure twenty years before. In the closing weeks of the 1964 Presidential campaign, Reagan, known then only as an actor, had gone on television to speak for the Republican candidate, Barry Goldwater, saying, "Already the hour is late. Government has laid its hand on health, housing, farming industry, commerce, education . . ."

When he finally won the nomination of the party himself, in the summer of 1980, he presided over the adoption of a Republican platform that said:

15

> For too many years, the political debate in America
> has been conducted in terms dictated by the Demo-
> crats. They believe that every time new problems
> arise beyond the power of men and women as indi-
> viduals to solve, it becomes the duty of the govern-
> ment to solve them. We seek to restore the family,
> the neighborhood, the community and the workplace
> as vital alternatives in our national life to ever-
> expanding federal power.

Good *old* American rhetoric. In traveling the United States,
Alexis de Tocqueville, taking notes for what would become
Democracy in America, remarked on the number of American politicians who gained control of government by attacking
it. "It was by promising to weaken it," Tocqueville said, "that
one won the right to control it." What was new this time, one
hundred fifty years later, was that Reagan meant most of what
he said and seemed to believe all of it. He kept attacking the
government even after it was *his* government.

As President, Reagan made a mockery of the contemporary
conventional wisdom that the country was ungovernable. He
put together and led an Administration capable of effecting
real change in the Government—men and women who dili-
gently went about the business of dismantling or disrupting
some of that government. His opponents and, probably, many
of his friends had assumed that a Reagan Presidency would
be something like the Presidencies of Richard M. Nixon and
Gerald R. Ford: conservative rhetoric, but liberal governance
in the New Deal tradition. The Federal Government and its
functions, it was supposed, would continue to grow (expen-
sively), and the United States would muddle through in its
noisy worldwide competition with the Soviet Union.

The Reagan difference—that he meant it!—confused less
certain politicians and commentators. Most, reacting by praising (and thus dismissing) the new President as a "great" communicator, missed the point entirely: He and his people *did*
things, often with Democrats in Congress passively approving
because they did not have alternative ideas and programs.

The personal-income-tax structure was revised to provide the rich with more money for investment in the private sector. Corporations got tax and regulatory relief, and Federal support in old struggles with labor. On the most important social issue in American history, racial equality, the Justice Department, the national enforcer of fairness, actually began to switch sides, going into courts across the country to argue against the discrimination and affirmative-action cases it had filed in the past. Huge chunks of the country, protected as national parks or preserves, were opened to enterprising reapers of timber, minerals and petroleum. And on funding for the military there seemed to be almost no limit—either in dollars or in the Administration's determination to impose America's will on the world. The combination of military spending and tax cuts produced, predictably, a staggering Federal deficit, but that, to Reagan, was preferable to increasing the revenues available to the Government in the future. (The Defense Department has never been part of "government" in the rhetorical world of Ronald Reagan. If a slothful self-seeking bureaucrat from the Commerce Department transferred to Defense, he became selfless and vigilant, a patriot above criticism.)

The new President was good with words, but better with dramatic gestures. A section on "Fairness to the Employer" in the Republican platform was not nearly as effective a statement as President Reagan's firing of illegally striking air traffic controllers, a move followed by the disbanding of their union and the allocation of millions of Government dollars to train their replacements. (Training new controllers, of course, cost more public money than increasing the pay of old ones, but Reagan's willingness to begin over was one of the many indications that, in practice, his real complaints with government often had less to do with its existence than with which men and which ends it would serve.) It was a dramatic signal to American management about where the Government and all its agencies and lawyers would stand in future labor disputes. Could ultimatums to other unions at airports and factories be

far behind? They weren't; the balance of power between management and labor was changing—with direction and leadership from the top.

And, in directing the power of government toward his ends,
this man in the White House was backed up by committed
cadres who moved into the upper and middle levels of the
vilified bureaucracy of the executive branch and began to
break up or gum up the works—deliberately and efficiently.
The Republicans, it seemed, had developed a sort of govern-
ment-in-exile. "Antigovernment-in-exile" would probably be
the more accurate phrase. Conservative men and women who
had been trained (and frustrated by their inability to control
the bureaucrats) in the Nixon and Ford administrations
moved back into their old agencies after four Democratic
years—and this time they knew how things worked, where
the files were buried. People and precedents were dismissed.
Staffs, staff reports, regulations and violations were routinely
ignored.

The "problem" was under attack. That was Reaganism:
a determined, systematic effort to reduce the domestic functions of the Federal Government by choking off its revenues
while at the same time diverting a greater proportion into the
military.

President Reagan, deliberately and effectively, made government the issue of his time. The American dialogue became
argument and debate over the role and function of central
government. Not for the first time. The debate of the 1980s
was the same one that has periodically dominated the American dialogue for two hundred years: distinct views about the
relationship of the private and public sectors, and, on an even
more fundamental level, the nature of individualism. What is
the relationship between the individual and the state? What
is the relationship between each individual and others—and
what is the role (or right) of government in influencing those
relationships?

In America in the 1780s, before there even was a United
States, government was discussed as a necessary servant, but
a dangerous one. The question of the inherent goodness—or

evil—of government was taken up in *The Federalist,* in 1787, by "Publius," Alexander Hamilton and James Madison, who countered arguments against any government beyond police functions by writing: "What is government itself, but the greatest of all reflections on human nature? If men were angels, no government would be necessary." A few years later, the other side was argued by an aristocratic agrarian, Thomas Jefferson: "Were we directed from Washington when to sow, and when to reap, we should soon want bread."

The words live: Should (or must) government actively seek to define and promote the general welfare, or should it be nothing more than a policeman, protecting property and person, leaving all else to individuals.

Individualism—the word first appeared in English as the translation of the French *l'individualisme* from Tocqueville's *Democracy in America*—came to mean freedom from restraint, but the argument continues about which restraints. Over the years, Republicans have tended to link American individualism to economic freedoms, while to Democrats it seemed to mean social and cultural freedoms. Laissez-faire versus live-and-let-live.

The first Reagan term sharpened those debates. If American voters in 1980 thought they were just hiring Ronald Reagan to trim the excesses of the liberal and generous welfare state that had developed in the aftermath of the Great Depression, that was not the way the new President saw it. Mandates are in the eyes of beholders, and the Republicans seized the moment as a mandate for the agenda of Reaganism.

By 1984, Reagan had made his agenda America's agenda— an extraordinary political achievement. As the election year began, the President had manipulated that agenda (and potential Democratic opponents) in such a way that even as its Chief Executive he could run against government, and Democrats would have to argue for it. Similarly, his attacks on the "evil" of Communism (and any other sets of "un-American" ideas) had positioned him to run against the Soviet Union and, in a different way, against the rest of the world. His opponents were left to argue for international accommodation, but would always be vulnerable to charges that they would accommodate in weakness because they questioned Reagan's huge defense expenditures. The Democrats were maneuvered into defending the most unpopular aspects of both "internationalism" and "isolationism." In fact, those words, like others in American politics, had changing meanings as Reagan and his people more and more dominated political discourse. In more traditional terms, the parties could no longer be defined as "isolationist" and "internationalist." The Republicans became diplomatically isolationist and militarily internationalist. The Democrats, wth a tendency to compare all foreign-policy situations with the U.S. military intervention in Vietnam, were becoming the opposite.

But Americans rarely choose their governors on questions of foreign policy. So, in 1984, Democrats had to rise or fall nationally on how well they could do updating Madison's and Hamilton's arguments of two hundred years ago that men were not angels and that only government is capable of enforcing fairness in a complicated and competitive modern society— fairness in taxation, and in the regulation and treatment of the millions of Americans who, whatever they think of government, turn to it for food and medical care or for guidelines and loans that give their children the opportunity to go to Harvard or Yale.

This was the way the parties looked at those processes in their national platforms at the beginning of the 1980s:

"The Democrats have shunted the family aside," said the Republicans. "They have given its power to the bureaucracy, its jurisdiction to the courts, and its resources to government granters."

"It is not only morally right, but also far less expensive, for government to assist children in growing up whole, strong and able," said the Democrats, "than to pay the bill later for children and adults with health, social and educational problems."

On national security and foreign policy, the Democrats said the United States was militarily superior to the Soviet Union; the Republicans asserted the Soviets were superior. The Democrats called for arms-control negotiations. The Republicans vowed to accept no agreements as long as they had any reason to believe that a military-spending gap remained. The Democrats talked of sensitivity to the legitimate aspirations of the world's poor. The Republicans attacked "charitable ventures" in foreign assistance.

Those Republican words became national policy over three years, and before you could say "lack of Democratic alternatives" the opposition party was projecting not much more than fear as its campaign theme—fear of war, fear of what Ronald Reagan might do at home in a second term.

On the eve of the 1984 campaign, the Democrats had done precious little to develop or unite behind policy alternatives, or to develop a new generation of leadership. There had been a deep economic recession in 1981 and 1982, and Reaganism seemed, for a couple of years, to be collapsing of its own ideological weight. The Reagan agenda, it seemed then, would be just too much for most American voters to go for twice in a row, especially when so many working people were being hurt by it—unemployment went over 10 percent, and the President's popularity was dropping.

Until the economy improved in 1983, it didn't seem likely that the President had the energy or the staying power to effect anything approaching a fundamental restructuring of the attitudes toward government and politics of millions of Americans.

Those attitudes, about the translation of ideas and words like individualism, freedom, equality and democracy into the day-to-day management of a complicated society, were best summarized, I think, in statistical studies published in 1968 by Lloyd A. Free and Hadley Cantril, under the title *The Political Beliefs of Americans*. National polls going back to 1936, they found, showed a consistent pattern:

> The majority of Americans remain conservative at the ideological level in the sense that they continue to accept the traditional American ideology, which advocates the curbing of Federal power. Yet, at the

21

practical level of government operations, there has been an inexorable trend in liberal directions in the United States since the New Deal.

In other words, Americans wanted to cut government spending, but approved of government social programs, beginning with Social Security. Harris Surveys taken more recently show the same pattern: a majority of 1983 respondents approved the idea of budget cuts, but three-quarters of those same people wanted no cuts (or wanted increases) in a range of expensive programs from Social Security and Medicare to direct aid for poor people.

That American contradiction was Ronald Reagan's target. He wanted Americans, the majority of them, to put their Government where their mouths were—to mean it, as he did, when they said, "Government is best that governs least." The idea of Reaganism from the beginning was to change the political reflexes of a working majority of the nation, to get Americans to stop instinctively turning to government with their problems. The method of Reaganism was as direct as the man's rhetoric: to strip government of the capacity to solve or even respond to those problems.

The new President attacked government in the name of the people. Attacking government is revolution, and throughout his public life Reagan relied on the rhetoric of revolutionaries. In his first Inaugural Address, he quoted Tom Paine: "We have it in our power to begin the world over again."

Ronald Reagan was a worthy revolutionary, a man convinced he could change the way people think.

CHAPTER III

THE IDEAS INDUSTRY

RONALD Reagan, for years, made his living as an industry spokesman. He represented General Electric Company on television and in appearances around the country from 1956 to 1965. Then, in a sense, beginning sometime in the mid-1970s, he became the spokesman for a new industry—a conservative "ideas industry."

Many people, including some of his best friends, will always see President Reagan as the front man for dozens of right-wing institutes, foundations and centers organized and financed by intellectuals and businessmen driven into political exile after the crushing defeat of Barry Goldwater in 1964. While the Democratic Party depended intellectually on the ideas of the New Deal and the hit-or-miss work of liberal authors and academics, Republicans institutionalized the business of political thinking and the marketing of policy ideas. In the twenty years from 1964 to 1984, the Capitol of the United States was

23

surrounded, figuratively and literally, by dozens of conservative institutions staffed with aggressive scholars, researchers and pamphleteers proposing and refining ideas like tax reform, and deregulation, and aggressive international unilateralism. They pulled together and honed a coherent set of ideas, a view of America and the world that was persuasively articulated by Reagan.

"The years in the wilderness" was the phrase used to describe those two decades by a key figure in the intellectual renaissance of the American right, Edwin J. Feulner, Jr., president of the Heritage Foundation. "They gave us the time to work out challenges to the prevailing orthodoxy." Heritage, financed originally in 1974 by a $250,000 grant from a Colorado brewer, Joseph Coors, was part of that and more, evolving into a $10.5-million operation supporting scholars and researchers who produced analysis and quotable quotes to help sell a new orthodoxy: the view of a great nation held back by too much government, and of a world in constant and imminent danger from Communist aggression.

"To Empower People," a forty-five-page booklet produced in 1977 by the largest and most respected of the conservative ideas factories, the $10.6-million-a-year American Enterprise Institute for Public Policy Research, was an important example of both the work of such institutions and their impact on national dialogue. AEI supported Peter L. Berger, then a Rutgers sociology professor, and Richard John Neuhaus, director of the Center on Religion and Society in New York, in their studies of "Mediating Structures in Public Policy." Their conclusions, based in part on the thinking of the French sociologist Émile Durkheim and, later, an American intellectual, Robert Nisbet, included: "Alternative mechanisms [to the Federal Government] are possible to provide welfare-state services. Neighborhood. Church. Voluntary Association."

Three years later such phrases began echoing through politics, beginning with the 1980 Republican national platform, which stated: "We seek to restore the family, the neighborhood, the community, and the workplace as vital alternatives in our national life to ever-expanding federal power." In accepting his party's Presidential nomination that year, candidate Reagan began redefining the theme, which would echo through his campaign. "Everywhere," he told the Republicans in convention, "we have met thousands of Democrats, Independents and Republicans from all walks of life bound together in that community of shared values of family, work, neighborhood, peace and freedom."*

"There were ideas in the Reagan campaign last time. That's how he won, on the strength of ideas," said an opponent in 1984, William Galston, an assistant professor of history at the University of Texas on leave to be "issues director" of the campaign of the Democratic candidate, Walter Mondale. "It's almost impossible to overrate the importance of ideas in politics. Things like 'supply-side economics' may have been bad ideas, but they were ideas."

The importance was such, in fact, that Galston's candidate, with the support of almost every important element and leader of the party, almost lost the Democratic nomination to Senator Gary Hart, whose most persuasive theme was "new ideas"—even if it was never clear how many he actually had.

Ideas, obviously, have always been important in political campaigns, but in recent years they have often dominated American elections, essentially replacing party identification as the banners under which candidates run. As the words "Republican" and "Democrat" came to mean less to voters, and "conservative" and "liberal" labels were aggressively rejected by candidates, politicians—particularly younger ones—have tried to associate themselves not with traditional labels but with a set of ideas usually presented as "new."

"The political system became more and more sensitive to ideas as party discipline became weaker," said Irving Kristol, editor of *The Public Interest,* one of many journals founded after 1964 with the avowed purpose of injecting ideas into public-policy debates. "This is an intellectually turbulent time

---

* No one, to my knowledge, connected that rhetoric with the slogans of Vichy France in 1940 when Marshal Pétain adopted the chants of the crypto-fascist *Croix de Feu* (Cross of Fire): "Work. Family. Fatherland."

in politics. The decay of the old consensus—the liberal consensus—was bound to generate ideas. At the same time, since World War II, there was a spectacular rise in media that were hungry for anything 'new.' So you have politicians desperately searching to find new ideas. Every member of Congress is looking for the idea or set of ideas to associate himself with—something to set him apart.

"It used to be that politicians wanted to be considered 'sound'—that used to be the big word," Kristol said. "Now they want to be 'creative.' "

Or, as Hart emphasized in debate with Mondale, to be "first"—as in "I said that before you did." And there are more ideas around to play as chips in debating games. Or perhaps it would be more accurate to say that there is a greater volume of information that can be packaged or presented as ideas. There may be nothing new politically under the sun or, at least, since Plato and Aristotle, but in a newer world of social scientists, public-policy schools, and computers there are certainly much more data to be analyzed and more conclusions to be drawn.

What, then, can be called—and sold as—an "idea"? The analyzers—academicians who have had some success in getting their ideas into the national debate—seemed to agree that there were three kinds (or levels) of ideas in politics or government. James Q. Wilson, a professor of government at Harvard University whose research and thinking on criminal justice has been influential with politicians of both parties, defined those levels in this way:

• "Regime ideas"—basic concepts about the role of government; for instance, the New Deal idea that government should play an activist role in the national economy.

• "Policy ideas"—the basic programs on subjects such as deregulation.

• "Partisan ideas"—the slogans of politics, such as "new ideas."

Robert B. Reich, whose packages of ideas on "industrial renewal" dominated the Hart campaign after appearing in

26

a book titled *The Next American Frontier,* classified roughly the same categories as "paradigms," "policy ideas" and "puffery."

Or: Themes. Policy ideas. Slogans.

Working backward, the slogans are the day-to-day stuff of campaigns. The policy ideas are the fillers of position papers and party platform—during campaigns, piled on tables no one ever seems to walk by—but, more often than not, they become, after victorious campaigns, the substance of governing. But it is themes, clusters of more basic concepts (which can also be translated into slogans like "Get government off your backs" or "Human rights"), that win campaigns. And move the nation.

"There comes a point and a time when politics and real ideas meet," said Reich, "where puffery becomes meaningful, where possibilities are imagined. The great candidates, like Reagan, create a framework of reference for their campaigns. You suddenly can identify with their approach to reality. That's when elections are won."

Reich, a former Federal Trade Commission official whose book was published in 1982 with advertising blurbs from both Hart and Mondale, was the very model of what could be called the modern "idea entrepreneur." Working from a two-chair office at the Kennedy School of Government at Harvard, Reich traveled back and forth to Washington during 1983 and 1984—often paying his own way—to advise three Democratic candidates, Hart, Mondale and Jesse Jackson. Policy salesmen like Reich—"the fastest guns in the West," said Wilson—often drawing attention to themselves through the Op-Ed pages of *The New York Times* and *The Washington Post,* are, for all practical purposes, the principal intellectual resources of the Democratic Party and of American liberalism. They use politicians as megaphones—or try to. If they get lucky, as did, say, Arthur Laffer, the young conservative economist from the University of Southern California who sold "supply-side economics" to the Republicans, fame and financial reward are sure to follow.

But, whatever the dreams of intellectuals, politicians and

ideas mix only a little better than oil and water. "Politicians are lawyers, usually," said Amatai Etzioni of George Washington University, who came up with the idea of "reindustrialization" for President Carter. "They think in tidbits." True, but the men and women who face voters also sense danger in real ideas, big and small. "We all want new ideas," said Nathan Glazer, a Harvard contributor to *The Public Interest*. "It's just that we're against them.

"That's what happened to Hart and George McGovern before him," he said, recalling that McGovern's 1972 Presidential candidacy was badly damaged by an idea that came through Lester C. Thurow, an economist at the Massachusetts Institute of Technology: the $1,000 "demogrant" to each American as a substitute for welfare programs.

"Look at the Democrats," said Etzioni, who was advising Mondale at the time. "Meticulous lawyers. Hard-working senators. They have no visceral feeling for what we're talking about: the themes of politics, the *gestalt* created by ideas. They don't understand that it doesn't matter if Ronald Reagan has his facts wrong. The public thinks at two levels above detail. Mondale doesn't understand that. Reagan does."

Whatever the reason, Etzioni and other liberal intellectuals failed to move the public. The conservative system of ideas became the baseline of the American debate in the 1980s—only twenty years after Lyndon Johnson's liberal triumph.

Conservatives wrote of 1964 as a political rejection, not an intellectual rejection—and they set about the business of creating an ideas industry based on a liberal model, the Brookings Institute. In the early 1960s, Brookings, with a history going back to small research centers founded in the 1920s by a lumber millionaire named Robert L. Brookings, was a small collection of generally liberal scholars producing thick and thoughtful books and lengthy monographs proposing and evaluating government programs. That research and analysis were waiting there when Lyndon Johnson decided government could eliminate poverty: Brookings was part of the intellectual base of the "Great Society."

Conservatives, in those days, could only sit and watch. The

28

destruction of Goldwater, after all, was routinely reported as the death of the American right. The reports, it turned out, were exaggerated. Conservative scholars and intellectuals had survived by retreating into their "wilderness." Two of the sanctuaries where they tended their wounds (and wounded) and tried to figure out what had hit them were a couple of small research institutes with budgets of less than $1 million: the Hoover Institute at Stanford University, an outgrowth of Herbert Hoover's extensive collection of military artifacts; and the American Enterprise Institute, a Washington operation with a trivial history of pumping out studies enthusiastically affirming Calvin Coolidge's dictum that the business of America was business.

"For forty years," said William J. Baroody, Jr., the president of AEI, "public policy had been dominated by a single idea: Whatever the individual cannot do for himself or herself, it is the responsibility and social obligation of the government to do so. The partisan argument was basically over which level of government would deal with which problem. We set out to challenge that consensus at the most fundamental levels."

That they did. Baroody and, particularly, his father before him—William J. Baroody, Sr., retired as president of AEI in 1978—recruited a formidable community of scholars, many of whom were also affiliated with Hoover, whose work and ideas, after years, began to be regarded at least as highly as Brookings' output. AEI was quicker, more topical, more useful to policymakers. Increasingly, Brookings was producing longer and more theoretical books, while AEI's writers—including Robert Bork, Jeane Kirkpatrick, Rudolph Penner and Murray Weidenbaum—were getting out pointed pamphlets on the issues and budgets of the day.

"To Empower People" was one important AEI product. Another, in 1975, a 112-page book by Weidenbaum, helped begin the national debate on "deregulation" of business. *Government-Mandated Price Increases* was Weidenbaum's title, and he argued that inspections and controls by Federal agencies were stifling American productivity. The little book became something of a sacred text to conservative politicians—and, along with Hoover Institution regulation studies, to some liberal legislators too, including Senator Edward M. Kennedy, the leader of the Congressional fight for airline deregulation in the late 1970s.

"Ideas are now the way you do business in Washington," Baroody said. "Not 'new' ideas, necessarily. Workable ideas. We're idea brokers. We give policymakers what they want and need."

"When they want it," added Edwin J. Feulner, the president of the Heritage Foundation. "The way to have impact is to get your stuff on the right desk when decisions are actually being made."

Heritage, just ten years old and just down Massachusetts Avenue from the Capitol, is the model of an aggressive, disciplined conservative idea factory. Heritage, by the late 1970s, was supporting platoons of young and, usually, very conservative political academics producing piles of powerful papers, from books to one-page position papers.

Heritage emphasis was on the short stuff. Heritage functions almost like a newspaper: today's background and analysis today. Within forty-eight hours of the shooting down of Korean Airlines Flight 007 in September 1983, Heritage had an "Executive Memo—KAL 007 Massacre" ready for more than four thousand members of Congress, Administration officials and journalists. The circumstances of the incident were still unclear at the time, but the memo listed Soviet "outrages" back to the invasion of Czechloslovakia in 1968 and called for insuring "lasting political support for strong national defense." Friendly congressmen and columnists immediately began quoting from the document—with and without attribution—which was the point of producing it in the first place.

Heritage also influenced Washington debate by supplying "testifiers," conservative academics from around the country brought to Washington to promote the research and viewpoints of the right before Congressional committees and Federal agencies. The Foundation's *Resource Bank,* a book published annually, listed, in 1984, four hundred research organizations and twelve hundred scholars "who share our goals of individual freedom, limited government and a strong national defense."

The conservatives also did not restrict themselves to trying to influence the thinking of today's decisionmakers. They were going after everyone from senators in Washington to high school debaters across the country. When the 1985 question for high school debate teams was announced in March of that year—"Should the Federal government provide employment for all employable United States citizens living in poverty?"—the Cato Institute, a conservative operation emphasizing libertarian views, began distributing a twenty-five-page paper titled "The Myth of Government Job Creation" to debate coaches and their young charges. "Government taxing and spending programs only *redistribute* existing jobs," argued economist Thomas DiLorenzo of George Mason University to the debaters; "taxation reduces the economic vitality of the private economy, destroying jobs there, even though jobs may be 'created' elsewhere by government spending on jobs programs."

"Marketing our ideas," "having an impact" are phrases favored by Feulner, who was once research director of the Republican House Caucus. Feulner, like the younger Baroody and David M. Abshire, director of the $7-million-a-year Center for Strategic and International Affairs, was an assistant and protégé of Melvin Laird, the former Congressman and Secretary of Defense. Laird, beginning with a series of studies he sponsored on Federal tax policy while he was a state legislator in Wisconsin in the 1950s, was a central figure in organizing Republicans to challenge the intellectual assumptions of Democratic liberalism.

Heritage, AEI and CSIS, which is affiliated with Georgetown University, were three of more than seventy-five tax-exempt research institutions that filled the landscape between the Capitol and the White House. Most, like those three, tended to be conservative operations supported largely by corporations and corporate and family foundations, offering offices, staffs and retainers to Republicans moving in and out of the public sector. The financiers included Exxon, Dow,

TRW, Chase Manhattan and the foundations controlled by Joseph Coors and Richard Mellon Scaife; the financed included Henry Kissinger, James Watt, Herbert Stein and Richard V. Allen, who received stipends and staff from, respectively, CSIS, Heritage, AEI and Hoover.

"The Republicans simply left us behind," said Senator Daniel Patrick Moynihan, a Democrat who is one of the few men of power who is also a man of ideas. "They became the party of ideas and we were left, in Lord Macaulay's phrase, 'The Stupid Party.' The Republican National Committee, under Bill Brock, even began publishing a quarterly journal of ideas. They also published a weekly magazine and sponsored seminars. There were ideas over there. The Laffer Curve and 'supply-side economics'—it's wrong, but I don't deny it's an idea. And we didn't have any.

"So, who ends up running the country? Politicians who know how to use ideas, that's who. The end product of government is laws—and laws emerge from ideas."

And the man who spread the ideas most persuasively earned the power to execute the nation's law: President Ronald Reagan.

CHAPTER IV

HOW MR. REAGAN BECAME MR. PRESIDENT

"THE Republican Party convenes, presents this platform, and selects its nominees at a time of crisis," began the preamble to the party's platform as Republicans came together in Detroit in the summer of 1980 to nominate Ronald Reagan for President. "A defense of the individual against the government was never more needed and we will continue to mount it."

Individualism packaged for masses of individuals: the little guy against the big guys. That may be the most powerful and enduring idea in American politics, going back to the image of a Minuteman leaving farm and family to stand against the British at the bridge in Concord. Thomas Jefferson, who never saw a settlement of more than a few houses until he was sixteen years old, gave Americans a democratic philosophy based on farmers and townsmen guarding land and children against the evils of cities. Andrew Jackson went after the national bank on behalf of the rough men of the West. Debates on states' rights began before the signing of the Declaration of Independence and continue today. The Populists in the 1890s fought the banks and the merchants and the lawyers and the railroads. William Jennings Bryan and Franklin Roosevelt and George C. Wallace each mobilized millions of individuals against "elite" institutions like Wall Street.

Populism—under different names, it has surged and eddied through America over the centuries. Usually it came from the West and the South, usually it was mixed up with down-home evangelical Protestantism, usually it was absorbed into the Democratic Party, building the political power of a Bryan or a Franklin Roosevelt. The energetic politics of suspicion—the suspicion (often right) of the little guy that he is getting a raw deal from somebody or something big—usually focused on "big business" as the enemy. But Reagan changed that. The President got where he is by redefining populism, by selling the idea that "big government" had become the real enemy of the little guy.

It was a neat trick, because Populist leaders in the past usually looked to government for protection against the big guys—preaching intervention in the economic life of the country to diminish the power and reach of big interests. George Wallace, as much as anyone, pointed out another way, though, when he rebelled in the 1960s against the racial liberalism of the national Democratic party and against "pointy-headed" intellectuals and bureaucrats. The importance of Wallace's 1968 Presidential campaign to the future of the Republican Party was spotted by Kevin P. Phillips in his 1969 book *The Emerging Republican Majority*. He predicted a coming "populist revolt" of new middle-class voters against new elites of "the corporate welfarists, planners and academicians of the liberal establishment."

That didn't seem possible to many, certainly not to many Democratic thinkers, because, more often than not, Republicans had been the party of the economic elites. The fellows at the country club were unlikely inheritors of the political

34

energy generated by the economic and cultural resentments and fears of God-fearing, debt-ridden farmers and workers of the world. A rich Republican with sure political instincts (and help from thinkers like Phillips) changed a lot of that in 1980. Ronald Reagan became a new kind of populist by redefining populism; he convinced enough little guys that the new enemy was not the private but the public sector. Bureaucrats. Planners. Waste. The problem was government.

There were, in fact, real similarities between the old Populists and their new imitator. Except in economic theory, the populism that created much of America's political history was never liberal about very much. With the exception of the more refined and positive attitudes of the Midwestern Progressives of the early twentieth century, pre–Franklin Roosevelt populism seemed, variously, anti-everything—anti-elite, anti-intellectual, antiurban, antiforeigner, antiblack, anti-Catholic and anti-Jewish. Populism was nationalistic, often to the point of xenophobia. Liberal intellectuals who mocked Ronald Reagan's appeal to "average" Americans should have known better, would have if they had remembered how the anti-business neopopulism of the New Deal overlapped with the xenophobic, anti-intellectual populism of the House Un-American Activities Committee and Senator Joseph McCarthy. In the endless American search for conspiracy and evil, populism has also always been closely tied to religious fundamentalism and public apprehension over cultural differences and any cultural change—from public dancing and loose women to television kissing and liberated women.

There is a strong, straight and very American line running from George Washington and Thomas Jefferson, who both feared that foreign entanglements were somehow evil, to the xenophobic rhetoric of Ronald Reagan. In the 1964 speech which made him a national figure he said, "We are against doling out money, government to government, which ends up financing *socialism* all over the world." That disdain for *alien* forms translated twenty years later into public expressions that there was no difference between South American countries and that the Soviet Union was an empire of alien evil.

That's the way most Americans feel, always have felt. The People's Party, in its platforms, demanded that "aliens" be prohibited from owning American land. And Abraham Lincoln celebrated his country as the last, best hope of mankind—a thought President Reagan repeated in his State of the Union Message of both 1983 and 1985 as "this last, best hope of man on earth."

So, beginning with a strong, ideologically conservative base, which polltakers said amounted to a little more than 20 percent of the electorate, Reagan built a voting majority in 1980 by uniting traditional enemies, the capitalists and a lot of populists, through stressing old values of God, nationalism and family. At the same time, he concentrated their attention on the new enemy, big government. He created a political world populated by bureaucrats, the deserving rich and the truly needy, welfare cheats and other ne'er-do-wells, "the average American" and—somewhere out there—"the evil empire."

The thing seemed preposterous. Ronald Reagan a populist? Government the enemy? The men who were officially called Populists, the angry members of the farmer and labor organizations that founded the People's Party at the end of the 1880s, were in fact little guys turning to government for protection and relief from the "greedy" and "parasitic" rich. Populist platforms in the 1890s included these demands: "We demand the abolition of the national banking system and that the government issue full legal tender money direct to the people." "We demand a graduated income tax." "We demand that the means of communication and transportation shall be owned and operated in the interest of the people as is the United States postal system."

But every one of those Populist platforms also called to the working-class conservatism that Ronald Reagan would reach effectively enough to get an estimated 45 percent of "blue-collar" vote almost one hundred years later: "Wealth belongs to him who creates it. Every dollar taken from [a man's] industry without an equivalent is robbery. If anyone will not work, neither shall he eat."

So, even if the Democratic Party's view of government as the great friend in need was closer to the principal political tenets of populism, Reagan wrestled them to the ground in the competition for the old feelings. He did battle with the Democrats on their own turf. He challenged their strength, their view of government's relationship to its citizens. "The goals of our Government must be to restore fairness and opportunity," House Speaker Thomas P. O'Neill, Jr., said in response to the 1983 State of the Union Message. Walter F. Mondale, Democratic candidate for President, then chimed in that Reagan was the candidate of "wealthy and powerful special interests," giving tax breaks to the rich, and was the servant of "greed."

"Greed"—the question of who is getting too much—was central to populist rhetoric, and Reagan immediately, and boldly, hit back at the Democrats, calling for fairness to what he would call "producers," the creators of wealth. The Democrats, he said, "suggest our program favors the rich. . . . As the political rhetoric heats up this year, there will be those trying to appeal to greed and envy."

Rhetorically, Reagan was the boldest American politician of his time, capable of conjuring up visions of the truly needy and the truly greedy and then blurring the line between them. He himself was truly gifted. He had blurred many lines on some of the great questions of American politics and governance. Or, perhaps, he had managed, as on the questions (or contradictions) of populism, to get on both sides of a few lines. He claimed, with some success, to be on both sides of one standard definition of American politics: "the ceaseless conflict between the man and the dollar, between democracy and property."* It was even possible that he had actually moved a line or two. "Realignment," after all, was the dream of many Republicans, members of a minority since Franklin D. Roosevelt had harnessed the forces of populism in the 1930s.

At the very least, for his own purposes, his own elections, Reagan, with great skill and some luck, had reshuffled the

* Parrington, Vernon, *Main Currents in American Thought*, 1927.

deck of Presidential politics in the 1980s. His economic programs had produced mixed success and failure during his first term, but the failures, including a deep recession with national unemployment surpassing 10 percent of the work force, had been in the first two years; and his successes were perfectly timed for the 1984 campaign. That made him personally popular when it counted, in the fall of 1984, but he was still, by any statistical measure, a candidate who had to overcome the handicap of being the figurehead of the minority wing of the minority party in a remarkably stable two-party system. He made it look easy, but Reagan's political triumph was scored against great odds.

The largest single group in the voting nation had already chosen sides—against the President. "Democrat" and "Republican" were still the words most voters used to describe themselves (politically), and, although polls had indicated some movement of voters back and forth toward the Republican side, preelection Gallup polls indicated that nothing had changed fundamentally in party loyalty between 1980 and 1984. Forty-five percent of voting Americans still identified themselves as Democrats and 25 percent as Republicans—and the great majority of those men and women habitually voted for the nominees of their chosen parties. (There was also no great shift in the numbers of people who identified themselves as "liberal" or "conservative" between 1980 and 1984. CBS, *New York Times* and University of Michigan Center for Political Studies surveys (and other polls) showed a 2 percent increase in the number of self-identified "conservatives" and a 1 or 2 percent decline in the number who described themselves as "liberal.")

The people behind those numbers were divided about like this by the pollsters: Democrats—minorities, government employees, academics and other assorted members of the intelligentsia, and union members in the smokestack industries of the Northeast and the Midwest; Republicans—the rich, suburbanites, managers and corporate executives, folks in small towns, and Westerners.

The rest of the voters were somewhere between the parties.

The largest numbers of them were white Protestant Southerners, often pulled away from Democratic roots by Wallace's
insurgency or by Reagan, or skilled workers in the North,
usually Catholic, many of them former Democratic voters
attracted to Nixon or Reagan or both. They were the children,
the grandchildren, the great-grandchildren of the Populist
voters and immigrants of the 1890s and the 1930s. Average
Americans.

Many of those average Americans could be described as
postindustrial populists—open to populism as redefined by the
candidate of the vaguely upper-class party their parents and
grandparents probably lined up to vote against. By the 1970s
those average Americans considered themselves part of the
great middle class. Religious and hard-working—even though
some of them were out of a job or, worse, an industry—
patriotic men and women, probably suspicious of both big
business and big government, and probably of big labor too.
Politically, they were required to function within a rigid two-
party system—American election laws are basically a contract
between legislators of the Democratic and Republican parties
to bar outsiders and insure each other's survival—so that in
election after election they were effectively restricted to choosing between two candidates.

The 1980s for many of them was a threatening, uncertain
time. Some places in the domestic economy seemed to be
disappearing, perhaps their own was next. Their great country's dominant position in the world seemed constantly and
almost mysteriously under attack. There seemed to be forces
beyond individual control pressing down everywhere. It was
a time for nationalism, a time for populism. Given the choices,
Reagan made it his time.

CHAPTER V

THE DEMOCRATS' FORCED MARCH

"RONALD Reagan won the Presidency because he had a vision of the future and the Democrats didn't seem to have any," said William Galston, the Texas University government professor who became Walter Mondale's issues director in 1983. "So, we have been on an intellectual forced march since 1980."

That was during the 1984 campaign. It was a humiliating and confusing trip for the men and women who had grown up considering themselves the cutting edge of the American political dialogue. Since Franklin Roosevelt's "Brains Trust" days, the Democrats had been the party of ideas. They had set the agenda for almost fifty years; now they didn't know where they were going anymore.

Mondale, the outgoing Vice President, formally announced in 1981 that he would be taking a year off to read and think.

It was ridiculous, but telling: after thirty years in public life, he wanted to take some time off to figure out what he thought. He emerged from his retreat to begin recruiting the people who would make up the core of his staff as he tried for the Presidency in 1984, hiring Galston among others. The young professor from Texas, who had taken his first fling at politics as a volunteer speechwriter for the independent Presidential candidacy of John Anderson, had the official title of "issues director," which meant that unofficially he was Mondale's "ideas collector."

That is the way politicians, particularly Democrats, have been doing it for years. They would hire someone like Galston to read for them. His job was to keep up with the books and articles of academics and other "policy entrepreneurs" who hung close to power (usually in Washington, New York or Cambridge), offering ideas and schemes to reduce poverty or increase productivity, employ the young, soothe the old and confuse our enemies.

Mondale, again like most politicians, preferred his information verbally. So part of Galston's job was to arrange "ideas retreats" for his boss. On the morning of the day after Christmas, 1983, for instance, more than fifty men and women prominent in their fields began arriving in Washington for a series of seminars for a class of one, the candidate. Economists. Historians. Writers. Former Federal officials. Professors on holiday break. People who cared for their country, the candidate or, possibly, a role or recognition in a Mondale Administration. They met with the candidate in shifts of six hours a day for a week, displaying their intellectual wares around a long table in a conference room of the former Vice President's law firm.

Robert Reich, the former Federal Trade Commission official with ideas about industrial renewal, was the kind of person invited in by Galston. In fact, the Mondale ideas collector had been the second person in Presidential politics to call Reich after he began publishing his thoughts in journals as obscure as the *Law Review Journal* of Hofstra University. The first

41

call to Reich, though, had not been from Galston. The first call came from Senator Gary Hart.

"New ideas," just those words, made Hart a formidable challenger to Mondale, who was the favorite of legions of party leaders convinced that constituencies, not ideas, were the building blocks of political victory. Hart's campaign took off in early 1984 only after the candidate was joined by Patrick Caddell, the pollster, who had been offering several candidates free advice, particularly a 120-page memo that counseled: "The Democratic Party cannot afford four more years of intellectual stagnation. . . . It cannot hope to be successful at the national level if it is unable to restore its primacy as the party of ideas."

True. But, all together, Mondale and Hart, and Caddell and Reich and the rest of the Democratic Party—including Jesse Jackson, who really did push different ideas, such as a foreign policy that transcended traditional definitions of interest and ideological competition by emphasizing strategies designed to meet the needs and demands of Third World countries— weren't really able or willing to come up with anything new. In the end, the chief architect of the Democratic campaign was again Franklin Roosevelt (with help from Walter Lippmann and other "progressive" thinkers of the early twentieth century). There was, of course, one other dominant figure in Democratic thinking and campaigning in 1984—the opponent, Ronald Reagan. The Democrats began by saying, in effect, that they were against what he was for. The President, it seemed, had reversed the recent roles of the two parties. The Republicans proposed now, the Democrats were wobbling between "Me too" and "Never."

After all the retreats and position papers and debates, the Democrats had no vision, or had too many. They were left with three themes or clusters of ideas:

NATIONAL COMMUNITY. "I learned to think of our country as a community," said Walter Mondale. "We are one nation, one people, a community, a family." That theme was lifted directly, almost word for word, from the rhetoric of Franklin Roosevelt, and, as a rationale for national programs, was a direct challenge to Reagan's decentralized litany of "Family. Church. Neighborhood. Workplace."

FLEXIBILITY AND PRAGMATISM. "A new generation of leadership cares more about solving problems than about debating ideology," was Gary Hart's challenge to Mondale. "A new generation is understanding and adapting to change." "Realism" was the word preferred by Mondale when he appropriated part of Hart's thematic contrast with the ideological rigidity of Reagan. Without the conservative certainty of the President—or solid programmatic alternatives—the Democrats attempted to make a virtue and a value of flexible initiatives and responses in such diverse areas as arms control, international trade and the domestic economic catch-all of "industrial policy."

DEVIL THEORY. Since more Americans have always voted *against* than vote *for,* the Democrats had to give voters something to mistrust—as Reagan aroused haters of "big government." Democrats had always been against "big business," but that seemed out of cautious fashion, so they were left with only the demon of Reagan—predicting small wars and more big tax breaks for the rich right after a Reagan reelection.

"National community" as a Mondale campaign theme was pushed by his chief speechwriter, Martin Kaplan. A Stanford Ph.D. in English, Kaplan polished up the cluster of ideas that had become part of the structure of Democratic Party theory just before and during World War I. In those days, Walter Lippmann, among others, celebrated the unifying and educating aspects of the national war effort. It was, Lippmann wrote, the end of "a nation of villagers." Later, the idea was more directly articulated by Roosevelt: "We have been extending to our national life the old principle of the local community . . . the neighbors [now] are the people of the United States as a whole."

But that vision of community (like Reagan's ideas) goes

43

farther back in American history than the Democratic Party. Walter Mondale, the son of a Methodist minister, commented a couple years ago on the irony of Ronald Reagan announcing his candidacy for President in 1980 by recalling the most famous line of John Winthrop's sermon to the Puritans approaching Massachusetts Bay in 1630 aboard the ship *Arbella:* "We shall be as a city on a hill."

Reagan adopted the words and the image, but Winthrop's ideas for the great city were much closer to Mondale's. "We must strengthen, defend, preserve and comfort each other," the preacher said that day more than three hundred years ago. "We must love one another. We must bear one another's burdens. We must not look only on our things, but also on the things of our brethren. We must rejoice together, mourn together, labor and suffer together."

"It is a conception of society that asserts no version of *triage* is acceptable," Kaplan said—government's role is to insure that not only the fittest survive and thrive. Mondale himself usually said it this way: "There's nothing more basic to the principles of America than that we are in this country and in this society together. We belong to one another. America is supposed to be a community, a family."

The "family" references in recent Democratic rhetoric began with Mario Cuomo, who was elected governor of New York in 1982. He used the word in the same way one of his predecessors in that job, Franklin Roosevelt, had used "community." Cuomo called the people of his state, all the people, "the family of New York." Then, as he became a national figure, the family grew. "We believe we must be the family of America," Cuomo said, "that at the heart of the matter we are bound to each other. We believe in a single fundamental idea that describes better than most textbooks and any speech what a proper government should be. The idea of family. Mutuality. The sharing of benefits and burdens for the good of all. Feeling one another's pain. Sharing one another's blessings."

Reagan too believed families should share the pain and the

44

blessings of life. But when he said "family" he meant Mom and Dad and the kids—you and yours, me and mine.

The Democrats were saying, "We're all in this together." Cuomo argued that the obligation and purpose of government were the same as any family's—including the redistribution of money, "to do what people can't do for themselves."

The Republicans were saying, "It's every man for himself—or for his own family. Talk it over with your family. Talk to your minister. Or the neighbors. Or your boss. Don't bother the rest of us. We've got our own troubles."

"The question," Martin Kaplan said, "is figuring out what is acceptable pain in a just society?"

"We're flooded with position papers answering that question and others," he said during Mondale's primary campaign against Senator Hart. "The difference between Mondale and Hart is that Hart bound the position papers and called it a book."

A New Democracy was Hart's title for the book he said defined his "new ideas." In the preface to the book, he listed more than one hundred men and women he had sought out—Professor Reich and MIT economist Lester Thurow were among those acknowledged—and then, for 177 pages, essentially laid out policy positions and options. The Coloradan called for "the public debate our country deserves" more often than he said which side he would take.

In his primary campaign, as in his book, Hart was better at defining problems than solutions. In effect, he was offering not much more than the idea that he was open to new ideas. He projected himself as pragmatic, while Mondale seemed inflexible—in his own (Democratic) way as rigid and ideological as Reagan.

"Industrial strategy" (or sometimes "industrial policy") was probably the most symbolic of the ideas projected as new by Hart. No one, including him, was able to explain exactly what that meant beyond some sort of partnership involving government, business and organized labor to make the United States more competitive in a world economy. "Cooperation instead of confrontation" was one of the phrases used by Hart, making allusions to Japanese successes with centralized, co-operative industrial planning in high-technology fields.

"The solution of the thirties will not solve the problems of the eighties," was another phrase Hart repeated during the campaign. Those words, in fact, were central to the credo of the group of younger Democrats with whom he identified: the "neoliberals." Disdaining many things "old"—"old liberals," "old industries," "old constituencies"—Democratic governors such as Richard Lamm of Colorado and Bruce Babbitt of Arizona and younger members of Congress were attempting to separate themselves from some of the weight of the Democratic past that weighed down "old" liberals like Mondale. That, however, was easier said than done. Hart and others tried to signal particularly that they were independent of organized labor—"the solution of the thirties." But in fact they still generally voted with labor in Congress, because unions, at least union leadership, were central to Democratic constituencies, old and new. That hypocrisy was one of the thoughtless (or idealess) inconsistencies that eventually eroded Hart's support.

Hart and his peers seemed to be trying to abandon the great steamship of organized labor, knowing that its membership and its influence on that membership had both been in decline for decades. But they still wanted the votes of the crew. When Hart went national, the AFL-CIO looked a lot more dynamic and powerful in Ohio or Pennsylvania than it had back home in Denver. So, rhetoric was the last refuge of neoliberalism in 1984. Hart found shelter but not victory—not quite—by saying "new," by preaching "pragmatic."

Whatever it was, pragmatism or new thinking, the Hart pitch and push moved the Mondale campaign around. "Realism" then became Mondale's attempt to match Hart's calls to a "new" pragmatism. "I will bring business and labor together to work for industrial renewal," Mondale said. "I won't blame government. I'll use it. Government does not belong on your back, but it does belong on your side."

Mondale was also maneuvered—into a corner, some would argue—by the more flexible foreign-policy views of younger Democrat liberals, both new and old. Almost all of them seemed to have had their views of America's role in the world shaped by Vietnam. None of them would use the phrase, but many of the party's next generation of leaders could be characterized as militarily isolationist.

"We are strongly internationalistic in the sense that we believe in shared responsibility in all parts of the world," said Governor Richard Celeste of Ohio, who had been director of the Peace Corps for two years. "We just believe more keenly in the possibility of peace than past generations did. Just because there have always been wars in the past does not mean there will always be wars in the future. The only real national-security policy begins with arms-control policy, beginning with controls on nuclear arms."

That kind of hope was reflected in the 1984 Democratic platform—written, not so incidentally, by many middle-aged men and women who had served in the Peace Corps during the 1960s. The sections presented to the delegates on "Foreign Policy" and "Defense Policy"—prepared by a committee chaired by Geraldine Ferraro, who would become the party's Vice-Presidential nominee—eliminated such 1980 platform language as "America's military strength is and must be unsurpassed." Instead, the draft platform emphasized phrases such as "A world of peace, freedom and justice," and "military force is of limited value."

That was the document prepared at the direction of Mondale—its foreign-affairs sections were significantly different from recent platforms of both the Democratic and Republican parties—and it was then modified even more to include noninterventionist planks proposed by Hart. Without public objection, the delegates in San Francisco approved several clauses restricting military options, such as: "The Democratic Party affirms its commitment to the selective, judicious use of American military power. . . . But he or she [a Democratic President] will not hazard American lives or engage in

47

unilateral military involvement . . . where our objectives are not clear . . . [and] where the local forces supported are not working to resolve the causes of conflict."

Mondale himself tried to have it both ways, promoting "realism" again. "The difference between realism and red-baiting is that we refuse to see the globe solely as an arena for East–West conflict. Nationalism, religious fundamentalism, the struggle against oligarchy: these forces are no less power-fully shaping the world." Meanwhile, his lieutenants cruised among reporters, telling them to remember that Walter Mondale was as anti-Soviet as Ronald Reagan. He wasn't. And he wasn't as militarily isolationist as Gary Hart. What he was, even before accepting his party's nomination, was in trouble.

The sad fact was that the Democrats had not marched far enough intellectually since 1980. Mondale had been so sure of winning during the deep economic troubles of Reagan's first two Presidential years that he never comprehended one of the things that Robert Reich, among others, had tried to tell him. "What the Republicans accomplished during the last fifteen years was a triumph of ideas, an intellectual victory," Reich said. "They shifted the burden of proof onto government."

CHAPTER VI

WHAT IS
A DEMOCRAT?

THE voice of the Governor of Ohio choked as he congratulated the Governor of New York on his keynote speech at the 1984 Democratic National Convention in San Francisco in July. "My father," Richard Celeste said to Mario Cuomo, "my father—there's a guy named Frank Celeste watching TV right now with tears running down his face."

There were tears, too, in the eyes of the governors, two sons of Italian immigrants who had come to America knowing no people, knowing no English. "I watched a small man with thick calluses on both hands work fifteen and sixteen hours a day," Governor Cuomo had said from the podium. "I learned about our kind of democracy from my father."

An hour later, two other Democratic governors met at a reception. "What did you think of Cuomo's speech?" Bill Clinton of Arkansas asked Richard Lamm of Colorado.

"Terrific," Lamm said. "It galvanized the crowd."

"C'mon," Clinton said. "What did it really say about the issues we're trying to raise?"

"Nothing," Lamm said.

"Passionate statements of what used to be," said Lamm as he left San Francisco. Described like his Senator, Gary Hart, as a "neoliberal," the Governor had been disappointed by the ringing rhetoric of Cuomo, and of Senator Edward Kennedy, Jesse Jackson and Mondale's Vice-Presidential nominee, Geraldine Ferraro of New York. "They all gave the same speech. We weren't ready to face the issues of the future—like international competition and productivity and confronting organized labor—so we celebrated the past."

The Democrats also celebrated themselves in San Francisco, as the Republicans would do a month later in Dallas. Conventions are the only place where American political parties actually exist. The nominating conclaves were an American invention. The Anti-Masonic Party held the first convention in 1831, and, a year later, President Andrew Jackson seized on the idea as a way of legitimizing his plans to replace his Vice President, John C. Calhoun. Jackson convened "delegates" of the Democratic Party in Baltimore in May 1832, and they dutifully ratified his choice for a running mate, Martin Van Buren. Soon enough, and for more than a century, the conventions were the accepted mechanisms for choosing national tickets. That function is still the official purpose of the conventions, even though in recent years the real power of nomination, especially in the Democratic Party, has been taken over by voters and elected delegates in state primary elections and caucuses. By 1984, the conventions had evolved into a week-long television show to project the party and its campaigners. And, perhaps more importantly, the conventions were the only chance for party members and outsiders to see who the Democrats are, and who the Republicans are.

Who makes up the Democratic Party? Who are the Republicans? Is there a difference? What do they look like? What do they smell like? What do they say about each other? What are the shared values? The shared assumptions?

50

What Is a Democrat?

In San Francisco, the Democratic organism, the party in convention, seemed to rediscover and celebrate itself as the immigrant party. What Cuomo and Celeste and many other Democrats focused on for an energetic week was their party's heritage as the political home and voice of generations of immigrants—the huddled masses seeking refuge from the poverty or the tyranny (or both) of Ireland, Germany, Poland, Russia and Italy, and, later, Mexico and Asia. The Democrats celebrated themselves, fairly accurately, as the party of the new arrivals of the twentieth century against the Republicans representing an older nation, white Protestant America. Whose America is it?

And whose Democratic Party will it be? That question was being asked by some white Southerners in San Francisco and by the kind of young professionals who follow leaders like Lamm and Clinton and Hart. But that was a question that couldn't be answered, or fought over, until after Walter Mondale ran his doomed race as the last New Dealer.

"This week was about the immigrant story," said Mayor Henry Cisneros of San Antonio, whose maternal grandfather came from Mexico to Texas in 1926. "I suddenly realized I was seeing history—I was part of it—when I stood behind Mondale at the Hispanic caucus on the day he was nominated. I watched him and thought, This may be the last time my party nominates a white male Protestant."

"You can't define the Democratic Party today without beginning with the immigrant experience," said Celeste, whose father came from Italy as a child in 1907, nineteen years before Cuomo's father came as a young man. "I arrive at my conclusions about what a Democrat is by trying to imagine what my grandparents were thinking when they left Calabria for this unknown country."

"My mother was the first Greek girl to go beyond high school in Haverhill, Massachusetts," said Michael Dukakis, the Democratic Governor of that state, whose father, also of Greek descent, came to the United States from Turkey in 1912. "The historic role of this party is to lift the new people up. If we lose that, we lose everything. This is not going to be the party of exposed brick walls and hanging plants and white wine."

There may be a confrontation coming in 1988 or later between Democrats who order Chablis and those whose fathers made their own wine. Some will fit both descriptions and may have to choose sides. For the rhetoric and the mood of San Francisco made it apparent that "neoliberals," or "future-oriented" young politicians like Gary Hart, were not at the heart of the party in 1984. The cooler young leaders who prefer discussing international macroeconomics to quoting Franklin Delano Roosevelt (or their own fathers) were outnumbered and outtalked by Cuomo and Celeste, Ferraro and Senator Edward Kennedy—and by Jesse Jackson. The black leader's rhetoric was essentially a variation on Cuomo's calls to "the family of America." Jackson's principal constituency, black America, was forcibly dragged into that family from Africa, mostly in the eighteenth and early nineteenth centuries, but he portrayed them as America's real outsiders, socially and economically the most recent immigrants. "We must be unusually committed and caring," Jackson told the convention, "as we expand our family to include new members."

Feelings of rejection of self or family, now or sometime in the past, was what seemed to be at the heart of the passion of the Democrats in convention. "Where I come from, politics is Yankees versus ethnics," said Carla McDonald, a twenty-six-year-old Hart delegate from Connecticut who came to San Francisco thinking of herself as just another Yale graduate student, but left remembering that she is Irish and Hungarian, descended from immigrants. "When Ferraro was named, I didn't think, Wow! A woman! I thought, Wow! An Italian Catholic!"

"We're outsiders—the Republicans keep reminding us of that," said Elizabeth Lara, a twenty-six-year-old Mondale delegate who worked for an oil-exploration company in Houston and is the granddaughter of Mexican immigrants. "People like me have to become Democrats if we're interested in politics. The Republican Party is exclusive, a country club that's

52

not open to me. You're supposed to be like them to get in, but I can never be like them."

Neither can people born black—or so an overwhelming majority of American blacks believe. "The Republican Party doesn't really exist for blacks, does it?" said Henry Ficklin, a black thirty-four-year-old Jackson delegate, a public-school teacher and pastor of the Mount Vernon Baptist Church in Macon, Georgia. "For a black, politics is the Democratic Party and the Democratic Party is politics."

The odyssey of Edwina Davis from Bombay, India, to Jacksonville Beach, Florida, and to the convention floor as a Mondale delegate was one of several similar stories I heard on that floor while speakers told their own from the podium. Mrs. Davis, a schoolteacher who married an American merchant seaman in Bombay, came to her new land via Philadelphia International Airport. The first words she heard on American soil were from a teenager at the gate who looked at her, then turned to a friend and said, "Oh, God, not another spic!"

With a group of thirty-one others, she became a United States citizen in Jacksonville on October 16, 1981. Twenty-two people in the group registered to vote that day, eighteen as Democrats. "We knew that the Republicans were the party of the white people," she said. "It's for the fundamentalists and the Moral Majority."

Some immigrants, obviously, do register and vote Republican, particularly Cubans, Eastern Europeans and Asians coming from Communist-controlled countries. But their numbers are relatively small. And Protestant–Catholic splits in American politics go back at least as far as the arrival of large numbers of Catholics from Ireland in the Northeast in the middle of the nineteenth century. In Massachusetts, a few Irish politicians still refer to Republicans as "the people who go to wooden churches," and there are still New Yorkers who claim that their fathers heard a Republican candidate for President, James G. Blaine, attack the Democrats as the party of "Rum, Romanism, and Rebellion."

Where you stand politically in the United States often depends on when and where your parents and grandparents landed—on whether your stories are of Plymouth Rock or Ellis Island, Kennedy Airport or the north bank of the Rio Grande. "I'm always shocked when I meet people who don't know when their families got to America," said Carla McDonald, whose mother came to the United States in 1951. "They're the Republicans. I almost fainted with joy when Cuomo mentioned Saint Francis of Assisi. I just never conceived that something like that would happen in national politics."

It did, finally. The Roman Catholic symbolism in Cuomo's keynote address dramatized the sharp religious difference in the membership of the Democratic and Republican parties. Just over one-third of all the Democratic delegates in San Francisco were white Protestants, compared with almost three-quarters of the delegates to Republican national conventions, according to delegate surveys by news organizations. Of the *white* Democratic delegates, 36 percent were Catholic (47 percent were Protestant), compared to the 21 percent of white Republican delegates in 1980 who were Catholic. (The Democrats, proportionately, also had six times as many blacks— almost all of them Protestants—and three times as many Jews as the Republicans.)

It's possible that those numbers could have a great deal to do with the future of both the Democrats and American politics. The immigrants of the twentieth century and their children and grandchildren, together with descendants of African slaves, have become the majority of the country's population. The face and the faces of the United States are becoming darker. The new groups also have many more young people than the great-great-grandchildren and other descendants of the Anglo-Saxons who came to the New World before 1900. White Protestants, once the majority of the electorate, now account for a little over 40 percent of Presidential voters, according to exit polling.

The change in America as the faces of America change,

though, could also be more apparent than real. The history of the country has been dominated by assimilation, not estrangement. How long, in generations or years, does an immigrant continue to be an immigrant? An Italian an Italian? A Chicano a Mexican? Mario Cuomo, for instance, was an exceptional Italian American of his generation—because he married another Italian American. Since World War II, 70 percent of Italian Americans have married men or women of non-Italian heritage—and more than half of all of them have married non-Catholics. If, after intermarriage, the other great indicator of assimilation is education, then the statistics are even more compelling: Italian Americans born after 1950 have the same levels of education as Americans who trace their ancestry to Great Britain. And perhaps Henry Cisneros, with a graduate degree from Harvard Business School, was his own worst example. He had crossed a line two generations after his grandfather crossed the Rio Grande. He didn't have to look exactly like a white Protestant mayor to act pretty much like one. There's a word for all these people: "American."

For some of those "Americans," assimilation is made official by rejecting family religion or politics—becoming a Protestant, voting Republican. There is great power in the immigrant stories—and the Democrats may very well thrive telling them in the future—but the fact that most of them can be told two ways was demonstrated during the campaign by President Reagan and an Italian-American physician named Joseph Giordano.

The President was cheered at the 1984 dinner of the Italian-American Foundation when he told the story of the family of a milkman whose parents had come to the United States from Italy. "The milkman raised his children as he had been raised," the President said. "They struggled to make ends meet. All of their money went to the education of the children. They put one son through college, and when he wanted to be a doctor, they put him through medical school. Because of their diligence, their son became a prominent surgeon in a great hospital. One day that surgeon—the son of a milkman—

55

saved the life of a President of the United States, who had been shot. I know this story because I was the patient."

The surgeon, the son of the milkman, was Dr. Giordano, the head of the trauma team at George Washington University Hospital. He had treated the President after Reagan was shot in the chest on March 30, 1981. When the President bravely joked that day, "I hope you are Republicans," it was Dr. Giordano who answered, "We're all Republicans today, Mr. President."

Dr. Giordano, who had moved to California, responded this time to the President in a letter to *The Los Angeles Times*. He said he was proud to be remembered. But he also said he was, in fact, a Democrat and:

> This is another part of the story. Although my father bore the brunt of the expense, I received low-interest government loans to help finance part of my medical education. The government social programs enacted during the last 50 years—and so frequently criticized by this president and his administration—played a vital role in making this success possible. In contrast to the president, who believes that social programs make people so dependent that they lose initiative, I feel that these programs have enabled people with little resources to reach their full potential.

The Democrats in San Francisco obviously believed, in the end, that these are their stories—personally and politically. The excitement of the 1984 convention surprised everyone involved, and most of it came from the passionate interchange between the delegates and their storytellers, Cuomo and Jackson, Kennedy and Ferraro—the immigrant storytellers. In fact, Walter Mondale, whose family, Protestants, came from Norway in 1856, sometimes seemed more than a little discomfited by the passions generated by the later immigrants from warmer places.

The heat was felt by some delegates too. Norman Fletcher, the fifty-year-old chairman of the Democratic Party in

56

Georgia's Seventh Congressional District, who was originally elected as a delegate for Ohio Senator John Glenn, said, "I'm sure this is a more caring party, but it's getting more difficult for me to sit here on the floor. This place is being run by two or three groups—labor and the blacks.

"This just isn't going to go over in the Bible Belt," said Fletcher, a Presbyterian who could not remember when his family came to America. "The newcomers are taking over the party. I'm not sure there's room here for me. Now you know why people like me are moving into the Republican Party at home. There used to be a time when none of us had ever met a Republican."

The politics of the South, the most Protestant region of the country, could almost be described right now as a race between whites deserting the Democratic Party—adding to the white Protestant character of the Republican Party—and blacks registering to vote as Democrats. "I'd call it a settling-out," said David Price, the acting chairman of the North Carolina delegation. "In my state, the Republican Party was a small enclave of white Protestants. Now more and more white conservatives are slipping that way."

He could have been talking about Norman Fletcher, who, in addition to being a lawyer and a state party official, was an elder of the La Fayette Presbyterian Church. Fletcher's peer group, his friends at the Rotary Club and the bar association, knew nothing of the works of Saint Francis and care little for the words of Jesse Jackson. "It's very easy to criticize without having any answers yourself," Fletcher said as Jackson spoke to the convention. "I don't like this."

So, in some ways, the new tension lines in the Democratic Party were actually extensions of old American lines—the Catholic–Protestant split of American politics was beginning to apply to the South, where the great white Protestant majority also used to be the great Democratic majority. Now those white Protestants were joining their Northern brethren in voting as national Republicans. In fact, the Democratic Party was so diverse, such a fair representation of the entire nation, that all American tensions were reflected when Democrats convened. The young–old tension of the Hart–Mondale contests carried over after the votes were counted. "Yuppies" ("young urban, upwardly mobile professionals," in the jargon of the day) weren't positive they really belonged there, either.

Carla McDonald, an "ethnic yuppie," was thrilled by immigrant stories and references to Catholicism, but she wasn't ready to buy all the politics of the storytellers. She had trouble relating to the dire tales of poverty and modern huddled masses. "The new generation," as she called her peers, seemed convinced that the future is theirs, and they cheered lines like these from Hart's speech to the convention: "The times change and we must change with them. For the worst sin in political affairs is not to be mistaken but to be irrelevant."

"Irrelevant" was a word used by another Hart delegate, Matthew Jones, a twenty-nine-year-old environmental consultant from Fort Collins, Colorado. He was talking about organized labor. "My grandfather was a union man on the railroads, my father began as a union man," said Jones. "I know the unions made working more human, but that purpose has been served. That's over now."

"I don't like the Hart people at all," said Dorothy Newman of Wyoming, Michigan, who came to the United States from England as a war bride in 1946, began working on a General Motors assembly line and became an officer of her United Auto Workers local. "The Democrats are the party of all the people—the working class—but these Hart types want it for themselves."

"Labor is going to have to learn to bend," said Carla McDonald when I told her of Dorothy Newman's feelings. "Unions have got to learn that labor is not synonymous with the Democratic Party."

They had all sensed the separation from unions that is near the top of the neoliberal agenda—it's on the Yuppie agenda too. "The young professionals I know are very open to Ronald Reagan," said Jones. "That was the choice for many: Hart or Reagan."

Walking that floor among the Democrats convened, it was not difficult to see the struggles that were coming between the cool neoliberals and the passionate storytellers; Lamm and Hart and Clinton might be in one camp, with Cuomo, Jackson, Celeste and Ferraro in the other. Despite that lineup of politicians on either side of the Mississippi River, the struggles might not be strictly geographic—partly because the immigrant-rooted politics of men like Cuomo and Kennedy could have great appeal among Mexican Americans and Asian Americans in the Southwest and California, and partly because many new-generation political leaders are trying to avoid taking sides. Mayor Cisneros, Senator Bill Bradley of New Jersey and Governor Bob Graham of Florida all talked to me in San Francisco of finding issues that link the proponents of "change" and the champions of "fairness." Bradley, particularly, thought the party could unite diverse constituencies by articulating a range of "workplace/leisure" issues, such as the retraining of workers displaced by automation. "We have to create a work force motivated and anxious to provide what the country needs, greater productivity," he said. "The Republicans will not consider that part of the political process, so they will leave the field open to us, as they did years ago when they did not consider social welfare part of the government process."

Fairness in a changing workplace seemed to be one of the several themes that might unite the younger Democrats who competed for attention at San Francisco. A more flexible, less confrontational American world posture might be another. (Such defense-minded young Democrats as Senator Sam Nunn of Georgia were conspicuous by their absence at the convention.) And both traditional and "neo" liberals were committed strongly to public education as the gateway to both immigrant opportunity and hi-tech futures (while their Republican counterparts pushed tax credits for private-school tuition), and on the idea that working women and women's rights were economic necessities whose time has come.

For most of that next leadership generation of Democrats,

foreign and defense policy are obviously related to the Vietnam experience. Gary Hart, for one, began his political career working for candidates Robert Kennedy and George McGovern—and against American military involvement in Southeast Asia. Views similar to his often separated the young from the old on the convention floor.

"To me," said Carla McDonald, "there isn't a great deal of difference on defense between Mondale and Reagan. They are both products of the old Cold War mentality." On the other side of the floor and many issues, Norman Fletcher was sitting alone in the Georgia delegation, shaking his head, saying, "I'll tell you something: President Reagan is right about the Soviets. I have no disagreements with the President's foreign policy. This is going too far. It makes me wonder what I'm doing here."

He probably won't be back. Fletcher left for home in Georgia saying that he still felt some commitment to the party and that he would vote Democratic—for state and local offices. "But," he said, "I can't go out and campaign for Mondale or this ticket."

Could he vote for Mondale?

"Well, I guess that's between me and the ballot box."

Matt Jones, the environmental consultant who was a Hart delegate, said he would not work for the ticket, either. "What's the point?" he said. "With this ticket, the Democrats have already written off Colorado. I've got to get back to my business."

But Dorothy Newman of the UAW put in every hour she could for the Mondale-Ferraro ticket back in Michigan. "I'd like to help move this party back toward the old days," she said. "I think we've gotten a little elitist."

Edwina Davis campaigned enthusiastically, too, for the first time in a Presidential election as a citizen back in Jacksonville. The Reverend Ficklin "preached Democratic" in Macon. Liz Lara in Houston and Carla McDonald in Connecticut worked for the ticket even though both still thought Mondale was a sure loser. (Miss McDonald was among several delegates who were already looking forward to a Cuomo–Bradley contest for the Democratic nomination in 1988.)

David Price worked for the Mondale-Ferraro ticket in North Carolina in an official capacity. But, as a political scientist at Duke University, he continued his studies of the "settling out" of white Democrats into the Republican Party. "All I'm sure of is that this is a party in transition," he said. "But I can't tell if it's renaissance or decline."

There seemed, for a few shining days in San Francisco, to be a renewal of purpose and of energy; then there was the campaign and decline. The old New Deal politics of Walter Mondale was an embarrassment. But the alternatives were risky, too. If the Democrats evolved into a party of immigrants and outsiders, many ethnics, particularly second- and third-generation voters who were economically secure, would almost certainly choose to identify with insiders and the older American heritage. They'll go with the Yankees. They'll go with the winners.

The group most likely to go that way were the young professionals. Ethnicity might have no more hold on many of them than any of the other things that make up contemporary lifestyles. The yuppies could split between the Democratic and Republican parties, perhaps even reconstituting dormant liberal Republicanism. They fit that old mold: culturally liberal, economically conservative. There were a lot of them out there, and a permanent shift to Republicanism by enough of them would change American politics for a long time. It could create real homegrown class politics. But it could happen. Some Democrats might welcome it.

"Not everybody, thank God, wants to be a yuppie," said Governor Dukakis. "The role of this party may be to continue lifting up the 'new' Americans. There are going to be increasing waves of immigrants—mostly Hispanic and Asian, but Greeks are still coming, too. I'll tell you something about them: Their children will be what we need, the Ph.D.'s of tomorrow."

"The future of America, or at least the Democratic Party,

may be like its past: the immigrant story," said Mayor Cisneros. "The country has always run on the raw energy of the
most recent arrivals."

They're both probably right. The problem is that many of
those new Ph.D.s will quickly forget where they came from
and be more interested in where they want to get to, where
the Yankees are.

CHAPTER VII

WHO THE REPUBLICANS ARE

"NUESTRA casa es su casa," United States Treasurer Katherine Ortega said in the keynote address of the 1984 Republican National Convention in Dallas. "Our home is your home"—this party is open.

On the floor below, Barry Jackson, an alternate delegate from Iowa and the co-chairman of the party in Johnson County, wore a red, white and blue button that said, "Republican Mainstream Committee"—the insignia of the small organization of Republicans who identified themselves as "moderates." A trail of hissing followed him as he walked by other state delegations. "Why don't you just get out of here?" "Go to the Democrats—that's where you belong!"

It was a long way from the podium to the floor of the convention that renominated President Reagan and Vice President George Bush in August of 1984. At the final session four days after Mrs. Ortega spoke, the seventy-three-year-old President was up there declaring America's "springtime of hope." Down below—during "unanimous" votes on platform planks and between disciplined cheering at every mention of optimism—lesser Republican leaders and party activists were talking of imminent winters of ghastly problems and hard times in the nation, and of savage power struggles in the party.

"This is all fine for a week, but tough choices, tough times are coming," said Senator Robert Dole of Kansas, with a certain tension in his voice, as the convention ended. "We're going back to the real world now—it's called Washington."

A more "moderate" (or liberal) Senator, Charles McC. Mathias, Jr., of Maryland, said, "Reality is about to intervene on this optimism. Ghastly problems—the cash of the Government of the United States is running out, and who really knows what kind of shape Reagan is in now, to say nothing of a year or two from now?"

At the other end of the party's ideological spectrum, Howard Phillips, the chairman of the Conservative Caucus, said, "The problem for real conservatives is not to be blamed when the calamities hit in the second Reagan administration, which they surely will, beginning with hard economic times, in 1985 perhaps, or in 1986."

The Republicans in convention publicly projected word pictures of a land of milk and honey—and television pictures of delegates whose complexions could be described in about the same way. The 2,235 men and women who renominated Reagan in Dallas were almost all white, three-quarters of them were Protestants, their average incomes were $50,000 a year and climbing, and almost every one had been active in the party for at least five years. The Republican Party was open to new voters, but there did not seem to be much room, or warmth, for new members. These folk had stood together for a long time, through the good and the bad, mostly the bad. They were a minority party and proud of it, convinced in their hearts that they were right all along. Still, as comfortable as they were with personal prosperity, they seemed unsure about the permanence of the political prosperity that Ronald Reagan had wrought. Not only did some of his policies, particularly deficit spending and a tendency toward enforced morality, make many of them nervous, but the whole thing sometimes seemed to be built on the magnetism and leadership—and the health!—of a man who would be close to eighty years old during his second term in the White House.

The words "Reagan's influence" or "control," as used in private conversations among Republican leaders in Dallas and, after the convention and the campaign, in Washington, were almost always euphemisms for "Reagan's health." Such conversations, and there were many, usually began with the President's obvious hearing problems and Congressional leaders' and reporters' perceptions that his work schedule was reduced and more carefully controlled after four years, possibly because all of them had less and less face-to-face contact with him than they once did.

"No one except his wife cares about Reagan's health more than I do," said the retiring Senate Majority Leader, Howard Baker of Tennessee. He had already calculated that his Presidential ambitions in 1988 might be little more than a personal quirk if Vice President Bush became President Bush before then.

"The battles for control of the party begin at midnight on November 6"—that was the line repeated across Dallas all week.

"We are committed to ideas, not to men or a man," said Newt Gingrich, a forty-one-year-old representative from Georgia. "What we do depends on what the Administration does in a second term. We're with Reagan if he's Teddy Roosevelt, against him if he's William Howard Taft."

"The young hypocrites," was Senator Dole's characterization of Gingrich and a dozen other conservative young members of Congress who helped write the party's controversial platform, with its provisions pledging to oppose tax increases under any circumstances and the consideration of a return to the gold standard. "They think they can peddle the idea that they've taken over the party. Well, they aren't the Republican Party and they aren't going to be."

65

Except for Ronald Reagan, it seemed no one could claim to have a firm hold on the Republican Party of the 1980s. Delegates in Dallas ratified, and loyally cheered, a very conservative platform, but news organizations' polls and dozens of conversations with delegates indicated that many of them disagreed with its key provisions and with some of the rhetoric trickling down from the podium. Those polls indicated that significant majorities of the delegates supported a freeze on nuclear-weapons production and opposed legislation prohibiting abortions—even though Republican convention delegates are generally considered more conservative than other Republicans around the country (as Democratic delegates have generally been considered more liberal than Democrats back home). More significantly, half the delegates in Dallas told pollsters that they thought the deficits incurred during the first Reagan term represented the single worst problem facing the United States—a big factor in the undercurrent of gloomy apprehension beneath the podium optimism.

Gingrich, for one, did not claim to have taken over the party—"yet," he might add. But their platform victories were convincing demonstrations of the energy, determination and political skill of the conservatives elected around the country in the late 1970s and the 1980s. Senator Baker and Senator Dole, who succeeded him as Senate majority leader in January 1985, and other more established leaders played down the importance of the document, but platform planks are a party's contract with its constituencies. The high proportion of the 1980 Republican platform that became law or policy during Reagan's first term indicated that promises and planks often mean more to governing than to campaigning—or, at the minimum, they provide constituencies with standards to which Presidents can be publicly pinned. Flushed with that triumph, Gingrich and his peers were just as determined that "the Bob Doles" wouldn't take over. The Georgia Congressman derided the Senator from Kansas as a "tax collector for the welfare state."

That, after the cheers and the balloon drops, was the way Republicans really talked about each other. Senator Mathias was called "a liberal swine" by one member of Maryland's convention contingent, Richard L. Andrews, a member of the state party's central committee. Mathias, along with three other "moderate" senators, was publicly invited to "do us all a favor [and] help the Republican Party by leaving it," by John T. (Terry) Dolan, chairman of the National Conservative Political Action Committee (NICPAC), one of the largest fund-raisers for Republican Congressional candidates. When Vice President Bush questioned such tactics, Dolan responded, "We are the Republican Party. George Bush is not."

What the Republican Party became, ideologically, during the Reagan years might be represented by a line from left to right—most liberal to most conservative—with Senator Mathias at one end and people like Howard Phillips at the other. Between Mathias and Phillips, moving left to right—which most Republicans did during Reagan's first term—there were Senators Lowell P. Weicker, Jr., of Connecticut and Mark O. Hatfield of Oregon, Vice President Bush, Senators Baker and Dole, President Reagan, and then Senator William L. Armstrong of Colorado, Representatives Trent Lott of Mississippi, Jack Kemp of New York and Gingrich.

But a more accurate model of the Reagan party, it seemed to me, looked like an atom—a series of concentric circles around an electromagnetic nucleus marked "Ronald Reagan." The President made the Republican Party his party in ways that transcended ideology. The test of position for Republicans was, in general, closeness to the power and person of Ronald Reagan.

The first ring, close to the center but not very wide, was the Reaganites, a small group including the White House staff and Vice President Bush. The next two rings were the orbits of the pragmatists—the "traditionalists" and the "old right." These included most of the party's Congressional leadership—Senators Baker and Dole, House Minority Leader Robert H. Michel of Illinois and his deputy, Representative Lott. Circling them were the "new right," from Jack Kemp to Newt Gingrich, aggressive young conservatives who saw themselves as new populists opposed not only to liberalism but to the country-club elitism of older conservatives. Then there were three wobbly outer orbits. One included the "moderates"—Senators Mathias and Weicker and young Barry Jackson wearing his "Mainstream" button. The other two, spinning and flaring together much of the time, included Phillips and Dolan and another fund-raiser, Richard Viguerie, collectively referred to, unkindly, as "the crazies"; and a companion ring of the "religious right," whose best-known figure was the Reverend Jerry Falwell, leader of the Moral Majority.

Pull out the center, the nucleus of the whirling mass, and the whole thing might implode. And that is exactly what almost every Republican I talked with in Dallas believed was going to happen. Four years after Ronald Reagan won the Presidency from dispirited and disorganized Democrats, the Republicans who backed him still seemed bound together principally by his magnetism.

"The post-Reagan era begins at midnight on Election Day," said Viguerie in Dallas, echoing the words I had just heard from Newt Gingrich. "It's going to be very rough," said Viguerie, the publisher of *Conservative Digest* magazine. "The bodies will be about six deep if the economy ever turns down . . . the Republican Party could be demolished."

Viguerie and Gingrich were as good as their belligerent words. On November 11, five days after Reagan's reelection, Gingrich wrote, in *The Washington Post,* an "open letter" to the President's budget director, David Stockman, saying: "You're becoming the greatest obstacle to a successful revolution. Your [compromising] strategy will split the GOP by Easter and mark Reagan as the William Howard Taft of the late 20th century." The next day, Viguerie, writing in *The New York Times,* went after the White House staff for "one of the all-time greatest blunders in American politics"—what he called the double-crossing of Republican Congressional candidates by the self-contained, self-centered Reagan campaign.

Viguerie was the more confrontational of the two—which was saying something—an angry man whose words were backed up by mailing lists he has proved could deliver contributions for conservatives' causes. He quickly concluded that

Ronald Reagan, as President, had failed conservatives, first compromising with the Republican establishment—by choosing Bush as Vice President and James A. Baker III as his first White House chief of staff—then selling out to the economic establishment, to "Wall Street" and the "big banks."

Periodically, Viguerie threatened to form a third party—a populist conservative party, organized with the help of television evangelists and local and state antitax organizations—to pressure Republican candidates from the right. "I don't think Richard Viguerie and some of his people fully understand our system," growled Lyn Nofziger, a Reagan adviser whose conservative credentials were good enough to make him a contributing editor of Viguerie's own magazine. "You have to control the Government first," Nofziger continued. "And they don't want to control it, except on their own terms."

Many Republican groups, though, seemed to have their own terms, and confrontation talk was common when they came together the one time between 1981 and 1987. Viguerie was joined in daily conferences in Dallas by Howard Phillips and Paul Weyrich, the director of the National Committee for Survival of a Free Congress. "Are Liberals Soft on Communism?" was the title of one of the conferences. One of several examples given of someone "who has been softened up by Communists" was Senator John Warner of Virginia, a conservative Republican who was reflexively anti-Soviet by almost anyone else's measure.

One floor below in the Sheraton Dallas Hotel and Towers, Terry Dolan of NICPAC announced plans for a fund-raiser at the nearby ranch of one of the richest men in America, Nelson Bunker Hunt, and distributed a "Statement of Principle" that included such lines as "We believe that if one is indeed hungry, there is always honorable work. We believe that aid should be forthcoming to the truly troubled, by a body most likely to know him by name."

Everyone for himself. You're on your own, buddy.

No one really knows how many voters actually identify with that brand of conservatism—10 percent of all Republicans is the estimate of William Schneider, the analyst of the American

Enterprise Institute for Public Policy Research—but they have proved they can raise money and are willing to use it in Congressional campaigns.

"I know people call us 'crazies,' and the party would love to dismiss us as a minor irritant," Viguerie said. "But you can't ignore people like us. We will make any sacrifice. We are trying to save this country and preserve freedom."

Down the hall from where Viguerie and I were talking there was a door sign that read: "National Coalition for America's Survival—Hospitality Suite." It is that feeling—"The world is coming to an end, have a nice day"—that makes Republican conventions more fun than they seem to be on television.

It was not only the so-called "crazies" who talked that way in Dallas. "I believe Western civilization is at stake here," said Newt Gingrich. "Political leadership is the only thing that can save it. I have dedicated my life to doing that."

Howard Baker, who was retiring from the Senate and was open in his Presidential ambitions, tried to deflect Gingrich's fervor with some humor. "I was young once, too," he said. "But I got over it." When I mentioned this to Gingrich, he was not amused: "Baker's a fool if he thinks he can wait us out. I made my commitment when I was a sophomore in high school. They can crush me, but they can't outlast me." Gingrich went on to tell a story about the French and Ho Chi Minh after World War II, comparing himself with the Vietnamese leader, not in ideology but in determination and patience.

Even Jack Kemp, whose party stature is higher and whose style is less confrontational, talks about politics and public policy as all-or-nothing affairs. "I'm convinced I'm right about the economy," Kemp said, reviewing his own advocacy of Arthur Laffer's "supply-side" economics. "But if, in a year or two, inflation and unemployment are at or near ten percent, then we will have failed. If the economy goes over a cliff, we're finished. Forget Jack Kemp. Well, I'm willing to take that chance."

"What a balancing act this convention is," said Merrick Carey, Kemp's press secretary, as we were leaving the Congressman's hotel suite. "The only thing they're sure of out there is that they love Ronald Reagan. Well, first we win the election, and then we get to the business of tearing each other apart—and maybe the country too."

"There are a lot of people in this party looking for confrontations," said Senator Mathias. "I'm not sure a lot of them won't be looking for a confrontation with Reagan."

Confrontation versus compromise was one of the fault lines of the Republican Party in triumph. The confrontationists—and there were a lot of them in Dallas, from Viguerie on the fringes to Trent Lott near the center of power—had contempt for moderates like Senator Dole. The conservatives looking to fight the good fight liked to say that the traditional goal of older Republicans was to lose as slowly as possible.

"If Dole or anyone else advocates tax increases after the election, yes, dang it, there's going to be some confrontations," said Lott, the forty-three-year-old House minority whip who sometimes tried to act as a bridge between the old and the new right, or between older and younger congressmen. "We're not going that way anymore. The traditional appeal of the Republican Party has not made us the majority. If you keep thinking like a minority, you're going to be a minority."

"You should have seen the body language of the old guys when I got to Congress in 1979," said Gingrich. "They walked onto the floor like they expected the Democrats to start kicking them around—and sure enough . . ."

The "old guys," though, looking back at decades of election results and poll figures, long ago concluded that the Republicans could win the Presidency when Democrats were in disfavor, but that if they ever hoped to have a majority party, a "governing party"—in registration and poll figures and in numbers of local, state and Federal officeholders—they had to accept the fact that many Democratic-initiated "welfare state" programs were forever part of a national bipartisan consensus. For better or worse, they had fundamentally accepted the notions published by Free and Cantril in 1968; they believed that a majority of Americans were ideologically conservative but practically liberal. The "old guys" may have been right, but there were going to be fewer of them in the Republican Party for a while—less of a buffer against confrontation tactics inside and outside the party.

In fact, there may have been a lost generation of Republican moderates. Senator Mathias, for one, believed that many young men and women who might have become Republicans in the 1960s and the 1970s—some of whom would inevitably have become activists and candidates—were driven away by Vietnam and Watergate. Many, he speculated, became Democrats; many just avoided politics of any kind.

Some of the moderates who made it during those years—Senator Robert Packwood of Oregon, for example—decided to avoid Dallas, giving up a round of Republican internal combat without a fight, which was an additional reason the 1984 convention may have been significantly more right-wing than the party as a whole.

But, if the ideology of the party was exaggerated for a few days, the culture of Republicanism was represented truly in Dallas. On the floor, a person knew instinctively and instantaneously whether or not he or she belonged. Everyone there knew that *"Nuestra casa es su casa"* was strictly for television.

That bent toward exclusion—and exclusivity—was a principal reason that the Republican Party remained as it had been for almost fifty years, the minority party, claiming the loyalty of something like one-quarter of the electorate. Perhaps Republicans like it that way. People *vote* Democratic; people *are* Republicans. Being a Republican is a cultural statement. Of all the statistics collected at the Republican Convention, it seemed to me that the most extraordinary was that 62 percent of the delegates had been active in party affairs between five and fifteen years. If you asked them, "What are you?" they just might answer, "A Republican!" rather than identify themselves first as New Yorkers or Californians, bankers or lawyers, Episcopalians or Catholics.

Being a Republican is not taken lightly. It means something. "There is a cultural mind-set," said Gingrich, who was a history professor before finally winning election to the House after two unsuccessful attempts. "Republicans share assump-

72

tions about proper behavior." That includes the company they keep. At almost every Republican convention there seemed to be a controversy over membership. In 1984, it was a 93-to-13 vote by the rules committee to reject a proposal to add 1,076 new delegates in 1988, a change that would have more accurately reflected the population by increasing the number of delegate votes from Northeastern and Midwestern states.

No. Whatever was heard about *nuestra casa es su casa* from the podium, calls to Democrats were for their votes, not their company. The party fully accepts few new members, thank you. Republicans are always inclined to check credentials—and question them. It should not have been a surprise that during the first Reagan administration the United States Information Agency was discovered compiling a "blacklist" of prominent Americans who would not be allowed to speak abroad under USIA sponsorship. Such people as Senator Hart, Walter Cronkite and Coretta Scott King, it seemed, did not meet someone's standards of "Americanism." That someone was probably at Dallas, and probably would have gotten a majority vote of confidence from the Republican delegates.

They have smug standards. "New Republican" is still something of a contradiction in terms. Ronald Reagan, John Connally and Strom Thurmond had once been Democrats, but they had long fit the molds of cultural Republicanism. "We have to learn to make people welcome, like blacks," said Senator Baker. "You just can't be on guard against them."

"Our instinctive reaction to newcomers is suspicion," Gingrich said. "Why are you here? Are you really one of us?" The instinctive reaction to Barry Jackson of Iowa when he wore his "Mainstream" button was to say, "Get out. You don't belong." Terry Dolan had the same message for Senators Mathias and Weicker and the rest. "Sure they want to open the party," said Senator Dole, "they want to open it to people who agree with them."

Public agreement—loyalty—has always been a high Republican virtue. There was real anger on the floor in 1984 when the 2,235 delegates realized that two of their number were refusing to vote for President Reagan's renomination on the Presidential roll call. What were those people doing inside the hall?

In fact, inside the party, Republicans have often seemed to prefer maximum control, even if that could be achieved only by minimizing numbers. The party has rarely organized locally to attract members. A confidential preconvention report to the Republican National Chairman, Frank J. Fahrenkopf, Jr., estimated that his party had "strong" organizations in only 100 of the country's more than 3,000 counties and was "very weak" or "does not exist" in more than 2,300 others.

Loyalty. Loyalty to Reagan. Loyalty to America. Right or wrong. "Loyalty is carried almost to tyranny in here," said one of the abstaining delegates, Paul Zimmerman of Pennsylvania. "You get just the whiff of fascism."

What binds Republicans together is that they have been accepted by other Republicans. Ronald Reagan was the nucleus that held the party together in Dallas. Patriotism has been what has bound the party together for almost its entire 128-year history. The President struck exactly the right note when he told the delegates they were "America's party."

"U.S.A.! U.S.A.!" was the 1984 chant, an echo from the cheers of spectators at the 1984 Summer Olympics in Los Angeles, but there was nothing new about the Republicans' claiming the grand old symbols of patriotism as their own. The minority party's history could be summarized this way: a political organization of rather exclusive membership that survived and sometimes thrived by managing to define "Americanism" for the rest of the nation—from the decades when all Republican Presidential candidates were former Civil War officers, usually generals, "waving the bloody shirt," through the years when party leaders found and defined something called "un-Americanism," to the days in Dallas when the party's platform was called "America's agenda."

The Grand Old Party has many legitimate claims on American patriotism or nationalism. That nickname, by the way, evolved from the Republicans' close ties to Civil War veterans organized as the Grand Army of the Republic. It was the Civil War, prosecuted by Republicans, that established modern concepts of the United States of America. Going back to the Old World, the word "patriotism" came from the fourteenth-century arguments used by a Franciscan philosopher, William of Ockham, to justify King Edward III's claims that taxes for defense of *communis patria*—the fatherland—were morally superior to demands for charity for the poor. William of Ockham would have felt right at home in Dallas.

After the Civil War, Ulysses S. Grant, the first of the former generals to carry the national Republican banner, summarized some of his attitudes: "I know only two tunes. One is 'Yankee Doodle,' and the other isn't."

One hundred and sixteen years later, the leaders of the party still seemed to know only two tunes. Senator Baker ended his turn at the podium with one: "We are a great people. In the last four years, we have shown the world just how great we are. We're *Americans*. We're proud of it. And we're going to celebrate it by reelecting Ronald Reagan for President of the United States."

Then from the same platform, Senator Barry Goldwater attacked the "other" tune. "Don't you Democrat leaders try to tell me that Americans don't love and honor America. . . . Don't you Democrat leaders ever suggest we are not on the right path."

Finally, President Reagan himself joined in, introduced by a film produced by the people who do the upbeat Pepsi-Cola commercials. It was truly a Republican movie, projecting a disciplined vision of America and American life. "Proud to be an American," went the song in the film, over images of weddings and churches and babies and flags. "I won't forget the men who died/Who gave that right to me."

The film was much more than an attempt to get some free television time for a Reagan commercial. It was a persuasive and emotional demonstration of what is at the very heart of Republicanism: defining Americanism; carefully projecting selected visions of America. Americans are, after all, a people who define themselves. Our patriotism has always been more self-conscious than tribal. Without a long history, Americans had to invent nationalistic legends. From the beginning, the

Republicans proved to be great inventors, telling new generations and new arrivals that being a good American, a real American, was very closely tied to the values of Puritanism and free enterprise.

There was one other thing that Ronald Reagan understood about the patriotism of his country and party: To an American, projecting faith in the future is a patriotic act. President Reagan proclaimed "the springtime of America," and it was unpatriotic to argue with that. As long ago as 1909, in one of the enduring American self-analyses, Herbert Croly wrote this in "The Promise of American Life": "There are significant differences between the faith of, say, an Englishman in the British Empire and that of an American in the Land of Democracy. The content of an Englishman's national idea tends to be more exclusive. His patriotism is anchored by the historical achievements of Great Britain and restricted thereby. . . . The higher American patriotism, on the other hand, combines loyalty to historical tradition and precedent with the imaginative projection of an ideal national Promise. . . . The American's loyalty to the national tradition rather affirms than denies the imaginative projection of a better future."

Walter Mondale would have been well served if he had come across those words during his "idea retreats." Ronald Reagan knew and understood them without retreating (or, probably, without reading). His greatest strength was an instinct for the visions and versions of Americanism, the ideas and words that have given millions of Americans something to live by and die for.

Those ideas had also helped create millions of loyal Republicans, and their version of Americanism was evoked when Trammell Crow, another of the country's richest men, spoke at the convention's first session. More than anyone else, Crow was responsible for bringing Republicans to Dallas, raising $3.9 million from local business interests to help pay the party's bills. His fellows seemed glad to cooperate with him— he is, after all, one of America's largest commercial real-estate developers, with total assets estimated at $3.5 billion.

"When I was accorded this honor," Crow said from the

podium, "my reaction was: Why me? I'm not a politician or party leader. I'm just a concerned businessman. Then I realized that ordinary Americans are what our party is about. . . . Let's make this convention a celebration of America's party, the Republican Party."

Crow's ideas were earnestly projected in interviews he gave that day—"I just came to realize that no one was going to look out for me but me"—and his words had a familiar sound and cadence. They could have been spoken in 1922 by Sinclair Lewis' George Babbitt, who was devoted to "the eternal importance of the Republican Party" and who proclaimed, "The sooner a man learns he isn't going to be coddled . . . why, the sooner he'll get on the job and produce, produce, produce! That's what this country needs." Or they could have been spoken in 1936 by Horton B. Wheatley, the banker created by John Dos Passos in *The Big Money,* who, in introducing his wife to a successful businessman who had served in World War I, said:

> "Anderson won his spurs fightin' for the flag, Mother, and his whole career seems to me to be an example . . . now I'm going to make you blush, ma' boy . . . of how American democracy works at its very best in pushing forward to success the most intelligent and best fitted and weedin' out the weaklin's. . . . Mr. Anderson, there's one thing I'm going to ask you to do right now. I'm going to ask you to come to church with us next Sunday an' address ma' Sunday school class."

Weeding out the weaklings was still a theme being preached with proprietary love of country in Dallas. "There are two kinds of Americans: the people pulling the wagon and the people looking for a free ride on the wagon," said Phil Gramm, who was elected a United States senator from Texas as a Republican after years of working with House Republicans as a conservative Democrat. "The Republican Party has put together a new majority of the ones doing the pulling," Gramm said, "the people doing the work and paying the taxes, against the ones who want something for nothing from the Federal Government."

Many Republicans have divided the world that way over many, many years. They are, after all, many of them, the descendants of America's Puritans and they have gathered together to make the party that has best embodied Puritan ethics, including the Calvinist notion that earned wealth usually marked a man among God's chosen. "Seest thou a man diligent in his business? He shall stand before kings," was a verse much favored in seventeenth-century New England. That idea, politically reversed, has often made it even tougher to be poor in America. Shirley McKenzie, a Miami real-estate agent who was in Dallas for a meeting of the National Black Republican Council, answered a question about poverty this way: "I'm not interested in talking about poor people. I think the best way I can help poor people is not to be one of them."

That was the right answer in Dallas, among the believers.

CHAPTER VIII

FINDING THE MAINSTREAM

THE first of the 1984 campaign debates between President Reagan and former Vice President Walter Mondale was held in Louisville on October 8, and the second was held in Kansas City on October 22. The timing of the televised confrontations was pretty good, because there is an old politicians' tale that says Americans don't focus on their campaigns until after the World Series in early October. Among the rights of a free people is the right to ignore politicians for as long as possible to concentrate instead on such matters as leaky roofs, tuition bills and the Detroit Tigers. For the millions of Americans who undoubtedly exercised that right for the first nine months of 1984, though, the debates may have come as something of a shock. They may have thought that the Republican President and the Democrat challenger were standing at the wrong lecterns and reading from each other's briefing books.

"We're taking care of more people than has ever been taken of before by any administration in this country," President Reagan said proudly in the Louisville debate, after twenty years of arguing against the excesses of the American welfare state. "We are today subsidizing housing for more than ten million people, and we're going to continue along that line." He also said, "A President should never say 'never.' But I'm going to violate that rule and say 'never.' I will never stand for a reduction of the Social Security benefits."

Then Mondale, whose career had been based on expanding Federal social services, emphasized that government largesse does have its costs. "I think also that the American people want a balanced program that gives us long-term growth, so that they're not having to take money that's desperate to themselves and their families and give it to someone else. I'm opposed to that. . . . The American people see this debt and they know it's got to come down."

There was no mistake. Part of running for public office has always been a race for the center—it *is* the center because that's where most of the voters are—but the 1984 scramble was more frantic than usual because both candidates had some distance to go to get where most Americans seemed to be. Reagan, after all, had spent most of his political career as the spokesman for the minority wing of a minority party; Mondale spent most of the general-election campaign trying to prove he was not a fringe candidate of some sort, insisting defensively that he was *"not* for new spending or new programs," and he *knew* "America must have a strong defense."

"Above all, I want a nation that's strong," Mondale said at the conclusion of the Kansas City debate on foreign and defense policy. "If you want a strong President . . . vote for Walter Mondale." And then the President responded by thanking the debate's sponsor, the League of Women Voters, for giving him "the chance to reaffirm my commitment to reduce nuclear weapons . . . my ultimate goal, my ultimate dream."

Since Reagan had attacked every arms-control agreement negotiated since World War II, it was not without a certain justification that the Democrat blurted out while campaigning in New Jersey a few weeks later, "Which Reagan would be President if he's reelected?"

Or, which Mondale?

The answer to both questions was the same: whichever one most Americans were willing to follow. It is rare that American Presidents—or successful Presidential candidates—are able to move very far from the tributaries of convictions, attitudes and prejudices that make up the American mainstream. After almost four years of strong (and strongly ideological) Reagan leadership, the President and his liberal Democratic challenger were looking at the country from opposite directions. There was a big difference between seeing a big, clumsy government as protector or oppressor, as friend or as foe. But between them it was, after all, the same country, one nation practically indivisible. Americans agree on most important things, as the candidates rediscovered with the sophisticated help of the extensive and expensive daily tracking polls both campaigns began using after the middle of September.

"It's not an accident that the two of them sound the same now," said Tully Plesser, a polltaker working for the President's reelection committee, three weeks before Election Day. "There has been great progress in day-to-day opinion-tracking systems. There is only one set of valid data about what America is thinking, and both sides have equal access to it."

The rhetoric of the candidates came together around that set of data. That is "the center" (to quote Plesser), and both Reagan and Mondale came so far because American voters seemed to be coming together around a consensus on the size and function of government at home and the stance of the United States abroad. The 1984 consensus, as it emerged in those confidential surveys and the words of the candidates, seemed to point away from both the Reaganism of the early 1980s and the updated New Deal liberalism represented by Mondale at the beginning of the campaign.

At home, Americans told the candidates' day-to-day pollsters, the welfare state created during Franklin Roosevelt's New Deal and expanded and democratized during Lyndon Johnson's Great Society was permanent, but it should be con-

81

tained at current levels. Such things as Social Security, national medical insurance and Federal aid to education at all levels were permanent blocks in the American foundation. Reagan was right in talking as if the New Deal and the Great Society were over—they were, but not because they had failed, but because they had succeeded and had been accepted as the baseline of an American welfare state. In foreign affairs, the same day-to-day tracking indicated, Americans were largely united behind both strong defense and an intense desire for progress on arms control, and they saw no contradictions in those positions. But they were divided, uncertain and arguing about small wars and big weapons in space. The people who were called, by themselves, "the last, best hope of mankind" did seem to be confused about the contradictions of wanting to run the world—for its own good, of course—and the expense and apocalyptic nuclear dangers of maintaining and expanding the military machinery which seemed the only way of impressing their higher ideals on lesser peoples.

"President Reagan was saying he wanted arms control. . . . Mondale was moving even to the right of President Reagan in saying he would be very tough," said William Hyland, the editor of *Foreign Affairs,* after the candidates' foreign-policy debate. "Both of them came awfully close together in their substantive positions."

It was as if the limits of the debate had been set by an outside force. And in reality they had been—by a public opinion that apparently began coming together in the late 1970s and continued through Reagan's first term. Reagan's military buildup from 1981 to 1985 was only an escalation of the buildup begun by Jimmy Carter in 1979, and, to a certain extent, the attack on government was an attempt to do what Carter only talked about in campaign and Presidential speeches that were anti-Washington, if not anti-government.

The most comprehensive review of the President's first term, *The Reagan Record,* published in the summer of 1984 by the Urban Institute, concluded: "The president appears to have led the country as far right as it wants to go."

The words and events of the late summer and the fall of

1984 sometimes seemed orchestrated to make the point that a new center was being defined by the American people, that the United States was moving toward political consensus. In the same week that Mondale declared his opposition to new spending—"no new programs"—David Stockman, Reagan's budget director, appeared before a Congressional committee to say that there would be "no more significant cuts" in programs for poor people. Reagan might propose more—in fact, he did in his 1985 budget—but Stockman's analysis proved fundamentally correct because the country (and Congress) had gone about as far as it was willing to go.

A balance may have been struck during the first four years of haggling between the Reagan White House and Congress over the size and shape of social programs and of government itself. Whatever his intention, Reagan did not succeed in dismantling the welfare state, or even significant parts of it. But, after years of steady growth, the proportion of gross national product going to the Federal Government had leveled off at about 24 percent. There was and would continue to be a struggle about the ratio of domestic to defense spending, but a consensus certainly seemed within reach during the campaign. There was little philosophical difference between Reagan's call for annual defense-spending increases of 7.5 percent and Mondale's call for 4 or 5 percent—and reading poll data, it seemed possible that even Mondale's figure might be unacceptably high to most Americans if higher military spending meant lower domestic spending.

Both men, after all, were working from identical sets of "valid data." The campaigns spent more than $1 million between them on daily surveys, according to Plesser, who formerly directed polling for the Republican National Committee. A Democratic campaign consultant, Robert Squier, added, "Polling has made a couple of breakthroughs in the past four years. Things like 'regression analysis,' which is a way of going back through questioning procedures, can pretty much tell you what actually 'cuts'—what issues or ideas actually trigger individual or mass action. Remember, this is being done every day in polling samples—four hundred new people are questioned each day, and the four hundred from three days earlier are dropped. Politicians now know exactly where the country is during a campaign—some of them know between campaigns too."

The technology is carried over to the business of governing. Many members of Congress do four waves of polling each year in their district, and the Reagan White House did between ten and twenty comprehensive polls each year, plus numerous one-shot surveys after such events as Presidential addresses. In that environment of targeted information, even opposing geopolitical strategies and specific international commitments inevitably converged—as they did again and again during the 1984 campaign.

As the President prepared for a meeting in October of 1984 with Soviet Foreign Minister Andrei A. Gromyko, to discuss arms control after years of personal and public hostility toward the Soviet Union, Mondale was meeting with reporters from *The New York Times* to say that he agreed with Reagan about the use of American troops in Grenada (in 1983) and would support military action by American surrogates in Central America if events and leaders there did not satisfy United States demands and objectives.

Reagan's moves and campaign rhetoric on arms treaties, after his years of opposing such agreements, could be seen as leadership or as cynical and empty political promises. But, according to his own people, they were an inevitable response to the public mood. Reporting on a national survey by the Public Agenda Foundation, a nonprofit research organization, in September 1984, Daniel Yankelovich, the foundation's president, said: "The American electorate is now psychologically prepared to take a giant step toward real arms reductions. . . . By an overwhelming 96 to 3 percent, Americans assert that picking a fight with the Soviet Union is too dangerous in a nuclear world."

But the same survey (or the same public) put pressure on Mondale too. Beginning with the Soviet invasion of Afghanistan in December 1979, Yankelovich reported, "The public mood was characterized by injured national pride, unqualified support for increasing the defense budget, and a general desire to see American power become more assertive."

The same public in the same period, beginning in 1978 with Proposition 13 in California (a state initiative limiting real-estates taxes, promoted by a grumpy populist activist named Howard Jarvis), also asserted itself in state and local "tax revolts." At the same time, in the same place, Arthur Laffer of the University of Southern California was introducing the phrase "supply-side economics," the idea that government revenues would be increased, not decreased by tax cuts. Laffer's notion that cuts would stimulate new economic activity and, thus, higher tax collections was promoted and legitimized by two Republican members of Congress, Representative Kemp and Senator William Roth of Delaware, and by the studies and statements pouring out of the new ideas factories in Washington.

"A lot of things were changing during those years," said Mondale's speechwriter, Martin Kaplan, during the campaign. "We're doing things we never did before, learning about things like business tax incentives. Liberals used to be for things because they were right. Now they have to be justified economically, to be cost-effective." One of the things Mondale did, a first for him, was pledge, during the Louisville debate, "No business taxes that weaken the economy."

In retrospect, it seems obvious that Reagan was the national instrument of that revolt and his 1981 Federal income-tax cuts were the climax of the citizen action that began at school-board meetings around the country. But if tax reforms capped Federal revenues (actually reducing them as a proportion of gross national product), they capped them at a different level from the spending consensus. Federal spending in 1984 was taking 24 percent of GNP, but Federal revenues were between 19 and 20 percent of GNP. The 5 percent difference was producing an annual Federal deficit that was approaching $200 billion a year. Laffer's supply-side tax cuts, enacted in 1981, had indeed stimulated business activity— which is what older economists applying the theories of John Maynard Keynes predicted would happen—but the projected windfall in tax revenues never happened. The exploding deficit was what happened.

If the deficit was the cause of—and the price for—the economic recovery after the recession of the first two years of the Reagan Presidency, it was the recovery, not the cause or the price of it, that dominated the national mood, the feelings of millions of Americans after the World Series of 1984. Neither Mondale nor the national press made the deficit a central issue. The Democrat would have been an unlikely champion of restraint. He had been for a very long time, as Reagan gleefully charged, a "Spend, spend, tax, tax!" liberal legislator.

Although Reagan himself had governed for four years as a "Spend, spend, don't tax, don't tax" conservative hypocrite, the press, the referees of the contest, were never able to make that point very well. That was predictable, too, because the press really covers politics, not government. The day-to-day business of running the government is judged too boring for most readers and it is only a little less so to many reporters— and economics was not only boring to many reporters, it was incomprehensible to most. Using adjectives such as "huge" and "growing" was the routine depth of press analysis of the huge, growing deficit.

Presidential politics has been covered as narrative drama since the publication of Theodore White's journalistic masterwork, *The Making of the President, 1960*. The book not only became a best-seller, the first of a series by White on Presidential elections, but it became the model for the coverage (even the thinking) of national reporters. The first book emphasized the strategy and tactics of the men (and, later, women) who would be President—and subsequent coverage did the same at the expense of analyzing records and programs—but that was not its greatest impact among the men (and, later, women) who covered the candidates. White wrote a powerful narrative with a beginning, a middle and an end. He skillfully used the techniques of fiction, building and revealing the character of his antagonists, foreshadowing the action so that small incidents led to major events. Every word, thought and deed, it was revealed—or would be—had a meaning and an impact in the unfolding drama.

86

White's imitators and disciples, hundreds, then thousands of them, began trying to do the same thing day by day, against deadlines. Character and conflict—or personality and contrived confrontation—became the central elements of primary and general-election campaigns. Later, the introduction of continual polling added a new element to the drama. The numbers created both events (crises) and an environment for the story, like monsoons creating and changing action in a flash of statistical light, allowing journalists to make continual judgments about the motivation and effect of their characters' words and deeds. Then, finally, television journalism came along, aping the techniques of Teddy White's children: compressing the daily drama into a minute or forty-five seconds of air time, heightening (and provoking) confrontation, kneading personality into caricature.

All the while, the new dramatists were missing the central point of White's craft: he knew the ending *before* he wrote the beginning and the middle. Lesser men and women were trying to write or broadcast narrative drama with only the slightest idea where the action was going. In 1984, the press created story line after story line that went nowhere, particularly in the Democratic primary elections during the winter and the late spring. John Glenn and *The Right Stuff*—the movies make another President! Mondale the Invincible—the best organization, the biggest lead in history! Then: Mondale falls! Hart conquers all! Hart failure!

Most of the talent, the slings and the arrows, of political journalism was focused on the Democrats. That was to Reagan's enormous advantage. Because of traditional considerations of responsibilities and territories—beats or "turf"—political reporters cover "politics." That is defined in the simplest way: people running against each other for public office. The Democratic battles were obviously politics. Therefore, the Democrats were politicians, covered with the traditional and rather healthy disdain of political reporters, who see themselves protecting the public from charlatans and fools. The President had no opponents—no contests, thus, no politics. Reagan was usually covered only as President, and only by the White House press corps.

In fact, for most practical purposes, Reagan was not covered; usually he wasn't even seen. When he did appear, a good distance from any reporters, it was in settings and circumstances of his own choosing. He had scripted his own drama for 1984, and there were very few speaking parts in it for reporters and correspondents. There was, however, a very large chorus of aides, Secret Service agents, policemen and, occasionally, soldiers to make physically sure that no reporters got close to the footlights or the makeup.

And, for quite a long time, it was in the self-interest of the press, print and electronic, not to make too much of the fact that they did not have access to the President, or really know much at all of what was happening at the top of the United States Government. A White House correspondent, say Sam Donaldson of ABC News, would have looked a bit foolish on the air when his anchorman asked what was going on if he answered, "How would I know? I can't get near the place." This, after all, was the same Sam Donaldson who was the centerpiece of an ABC advertising campaign under the headline "TO GET MORE ACCURATE COVERAGE OF THE WHITE HOUSE, YOU'D HAVE TO LIVE THERE."

Well, for all the press knew for long periods of time, no one lived there. "I seldom see Ronald Reagan," Donaldson said once, off camera. "And quite often when I do see him, it is at such a distance that I really need to look (later) at the videotape made with a long lens to take a close look at his face and expressions."

"The people elected the President to determine the agenda, not the media," said Michael Deaver, a former public-relations executive who was Reagan's personal assistant. He was in the process of announcing that Reagan would not respond to questions shouted by reporters when they were allowed to watch the President at "photo opportunities"—meeting with foreign dignitaries, boarding helicopters, kissing babies, that sort of thing. He and others also made it clear that if reporters violated the so-called "Deaver rule" of silence they could and would be barred even from such glances of the mighty.

The man had a point. The President did it his way—holding

press conferences only once every couple of months—and discovered that the bigmouths of the press were likely to stay shut to protect their own images as thoughtful folk sitting around the Oval Office at night chatting with the main man. The thought of letting Reagan be Reagan and sending all their high-powered talent out to see what the Administration was actually doing in all those buildings along Washington's marbled avenues apparently never occurred to most of the people running American television and newspapers.

With that background—and the press far in back of the protected President—it was quite a shock when Reagan the Uncovered came across as Reagan the Unhinged during the debates in Louisville and Kansas City. Walter Mondale clobbered the President in debate, showing a clearer and more comprehensive grasp of governing issues along with an exceptional ability, when compared with Reagan, to complete sentences he began. The President embarrassed himself, but he humiliated the press. Where had we been?

The Reagan who appeared on television from Louisville and Kansas City seemed a different person from the almost mythical figure, the "Great Communicator," Americans had been reading and hearing about from Washington and Santa Barbara for more than three years. The shock the morning after the first debate in Louisville was a public magnification of the private doubts Republican leaders had shared in Dallas. The public had been fundamentally ignorant of all that, and saw their seventy-three-year-old President as a seventy-three-year-old man for the first time. At times he seemed almost pathetic in combat with a younger, more vigorous man. Was the press also ignorant all along? Or was the press arrogant, too proud to let on that reporters might as well have been peering in at the White House through the wrought-iron fence along Pennsylvania Avenue?

It was pride wounded now. But the reaction of the press, after Louisville, was not particularly damaging to the President or his campaign. "Manipulation" grew into a story line, with correspondents enthusiastically competing to describe how they were being used by the White House. It was as if, having been cast as bit players this time, reporters were determined to reassert their own importance by demonstrating how much effort was being expended to manipulate them. I watched in wonder one night as the best political reporters in the country—from *The New York Times, The Washington Post* and *The Wall Street Journal*—gathered on *The MacNeil/Lehrer News Hour* on public television. The topic of the hour was, "What's wrong with the Mondale campaign?" The boys on the bus remarked that the Democratic candidate, unlike President Reagan, didn't focus on a single theme each day. Sometimes, they said, Mondale even talked to reporters, giving them several things to write or think about on the same day.

If the President's bad night in Louisville put the press publicly in its place—outside the fence, the back of the bus—it also put into perspective one of the themes of 1984 campaign coverage: that the impending Reagan triumph was one of personality rather than one of ideas and accomplishment. "Great communicator . . . nice guy . . . strong man . . . Teflon President"—none of the clichés of coverage was true that night. The President was none of those things. He was hesitant and confused, as he would be again in Kansas City. But he prevailed. Perhaps he could have won reelection just by repeating some of the few complete sentences he managed to get out early in the first debate: "We have reduced inflation to about a third of what it was. . . . The interest rates have gone down about nine or ten points. . . . In the last twenty-one months, more than six million people have gotten jobs."

Without complex sentences or reasoning, President Reagan argued, credibly, that his first term was a success and that he deserved reelection. The government, he said, was working better than it had worked when he came into office—and most people believed him. Achievement and credibility were infinitely more important to Ronald Reagan and voters in 1984 than was personality.

But in claiming first-term success, the President also conceded a great deal ideologically. Government was working well, he said, and he *was* the government. His victory, in some ways, was the high-water mark of the tides that carried him into the White House in January of 1981.

In a working democracy, movements create their own coun-
terforces, and some of the currents of victory in 1980 were
getting a little sluggish in 1984. The Urban Institute, which
did two studies of the workings and impact of the administration during Reagan's first term, published its first volume in
late 1982 under the title *The Reagan Experiment* and talked
of a "Reagan revolution." But the second volume, published in
1984, was called simply *The Reagan Record,* and the editors,
John J. Palmer and Isabel V. Sawhill, concluded: "What must
be understood is that it has been revolutionary in purpose but
evolutionary in practice . . ." and "only partially successful."
The Reagan "revolution," the authors decided, was over within
three years.

The American welfare state, the product of the revolution
of Franklin D. Roosevelt, had survived. President Reagan was
just the guy hired to rationalize that intricate system of state
supports.

Reagan, like Roosevelt, brought most of America together,
reasserting certain American assumptions and, at least for a
time, making most Americans share them: optimism about the
American future; the economic virtuosity sparked by free enterprise; and, ironically, the legitimacy of government.

The Republican was elected after (and possibly because) a
Democratic President, Jimmy Carter, had declared political
and governmental bankruptcy. In what became known as his
"malaise" speech of August 15, 1979—although he never actually used that word—Carter said, "I want to talk to you right
now about a fundamental threat to American democracy.
. . . We can see this crisis in the growing doubt about the
meaning of our own lives and in the loss of unity of purpose
for our nation. . . . Our people are losing that faith."*

That remarkable speech gave Reagan the opportunity—the

* It was one of the many ironies of Walter Mondale's image
as a man without faith in the American future that he, as Vice President,
had tried to persuade President Carter not to give the "malaise" speech.
Mondale thought it was substantively wrong and politically foolish. The
great champion of "malaise" was, of all people, Patrick Caddell, Carter's
pollster, who, in 1984, would orchestrate Gary Hart's portrayal of Mondale
as a pessimistic man of the past.

obligation, really—to compare himself to the Democrat he always said was his hero, Franklin Delano Roosevelt. In 1979 the country, democracy itself, was at risk. The President said so. It was something like 1932, when Roosevelt was first elected. Then, capitalism itself was at risk. And, in some ways, Reagan played a Presidential role that parallels Roosevelt's. The great Democratic President dealt with a breakdown of the nation's economic confidence; the Republican was handed that declaration of political bankruptcy.

"We found when we came to Washington in 1933, that the business and industry of the nation were like a train which had gone off the rails into a ditch," President Roosevelt said in a campaign speech in Chicago on October 14, 1936. "It was this Administration which saved the system of private profit and free enterprise after it had been dragged to the brink of ruin by these same leaders who now try to scare you."

President Reagan could not make quite so dramatic a claim about politics and government. But national polls did show a steady rise in confidence in government during Reagan's first administration.

If Roosevelt saved American business and industry or, at least, restored public confidence in their fundamental soundness (all the while attacking many business leaders), he then got down to the serious work of reforming commerce and shaping what kind of free-enterprise system we would have—the one we have right now. Reagan restored a good deal of American confidence in government in the process of trying, with limited success, to redefine its shape and size. The tendency toward consensus, rather than a confrontation of visions, during the 1984 campaign demonstrated more than one candidate's popularity or another's failings. The consensus of 1984 seemed to be the national gathering that would begin producing new decisions and directions—old liberalism and old conservatism came together in fundamental ways.

CHAPTER IX

THE POLITICS OF INDIVIDUALISM

"HERE in America the people are in charge," President Reagan said on Election Night, November 8, 1984, claiming his huge victory over Walter Mondale. The President won almost 60 percent of the vote; the challenger carried only one of the fifty states, his own, Minnesota.

The people did seem to know exactly what they were doing that Tuesday. They split their tickets—reelecting Reagan, but electing a Congress almost certain to check Reaganism. That didn't happen because Ronald Reagan was such a great guy that even voters who disagreed with him couldn't resist voting for him. He was just as personable in 1981 and 1982 when he regularly ran far behind any Democrats in the trial heats of national polls—and it didn't happen just because Reagan was terrific on television. Martin Kaplan, Mondale's speechwriter, cracked bitterly, on the morning after, that the only candidates who could have beaten old actor Reagan were another actor or a television anchorman: "Robert Redford or Walter Cronkite." He was trying to joke through his tears, but the line was another indication that the Democrats, at least some of them in high places, never really knew what hit them. People judged Reagan not as a performer but as President and they decided he deserved another term. But they tried to give it to him on *their terms*.

Reagan had come into the Oval Office at a time when the man in it, Jimmy Carter, was declaring political bankruptcy and important voices outside it, in the press and the academy, were decrying "the end of leadership." They were all wrong. The new President made the system work. He was leading, regardless of whether or not you agreed with where he was going. The leader was an extraordinary man. He worked only a few hours a day—outraging those who apparently believed Presidents should be paid by the hour rather than for their judgment—but that was all he had to do, because: he knew what he believed in and what he wanted to try to do; he knew how to get other people to do things for him, often whether they wanted to do them or not; and he knew how to communicate his goals as part of an overall vision of what America was and could be.

If he hadn't done all he had said he would, he had done a great deal of it—and had tried to do more before being stopped. And, at least in the short run, which is what elections are about, what he did well worked well enough for most of the people most of the time. Here, the majority rules. The President was rewarded for the tasks accomplished, and, at the same time, he was being cautioned not to go much further than the people, not to push too far beyond the limits of national consensus.

And Reagan's vote was very much a national vote—or, to be more accurate, a national white vote. Mondale, ironically, was right in some of his perceptions of national community: Americans, for most practical purposes, including the winning of the votes, have become one people, the same people in different places. Ironically, the Democrat, making the national

94

argument intellectually, had then campaigned not to all Americans but to groups of Americans. The President, while arguing for empowering intermediary groups, had struck campaign themes for all Americans, the nation.

Mondale's collapse, then, may have been more political than intellectual—many of the Democrat's ideas may have been old, but they were part of the consensus, the nation's shared assumptions. But the political tactics of dividing the nation into narrow constituencies failed as the President reached individuals in every region and imaginable demographic category with themes of American nationhood.

Television only transmitted those themes, for an instant freezing the mobile nation—reaching the ironworker in Cleveland at the same moment as the young wife in San Diego, then reaching them again when the ironworker had moved to San Diego and the wife had become a divorcee in Austin. There were no "local" events in 1984, or very few, and the Hart campaign was a dramatic, jarring example of that. There was not much point in arguing that national political decisions were accumulations of local decisions when Senator Hart, who became a national figure in just about ten days, could compete effectively against Mondale in places like Maine and Alabama without having campaigned in them. He was little more than a wiggly face on television or a cartoon on the cover of *Time,* while Mondale had been campaigning in those places for two years. But Hart's national "presence" was as real and as accepted as Mondale's and the new candidate won as many votes as the old one in those places.

The Mondale campaign had been called a "juggernaut" as it rolled across the country month after month in 1983 and early 1984 organizing the United States as if it were a series of regions, states, counties, cities, towns and precincts, one by one. Those maps of America covered with colored pins were swept aside because, more and more, it didn't matter where an American lived. The President certainly understood that. Reagan's neighborhood was television; dismissing him or attacking him for being good on television was like making fun of Abraham Lincoln for being an effective debater. America lives on television; the neighbors liked Reagan. Talking about the national neighborhood on the Tuesday night Hart defeated Mondale in the California Democratic primary, a West Los Angeles lawyer named Alan Friedman turned to me and said, "You know, I probably have more in common with a lawyer in Westchester County, New York, than I have with my next-door neighbor." If, he might have added, he knew his next-door neighbor.

National socialization was a reason that Republican politics of assimilation worked—"If you want to be an American, you have to be like us!"—even as the pool of white Protestants declined as a percentage of the national population. Well-publicized and well-meaning movements and campaigns to celebrate ethnicity—or regionalism or localism—were, at their most serious, romantic (or commercial) rearguard actions against the inevitable, the mobile homogenization, the "Americanization" coming through the television, into local airports and along superhighways.

Ideas travel fast, and America is a set of ideas, shared assumptions. Americans redefine themselves by emphasizing the present. You may love New York and proclaim your Italian heritage, but your son or daughter will probably move to Bakersfield, California, or someplace like that. The 1980 census data showing that the great majority of Italian Americans now marry non-Italians was cited by one scholar to argue that the selection of Geraldine Ferraro as a candidate for Vice President indicated that "ethnicity was not gaining, but rather is losing its potency as a social force." The researcher, Richard Alba, director of the Center for Social Demographic Analysis at the State University of New York, concluded:

> Increasingly, for younger Italians and others of European ancestry, ethnicity is a marginal ingredient in lifestyle, rather than an irrevocable fact of birth. It is doubtful that in the competition for votes, it can stand up against other strong pressures on voters, such as party affiliation or issues like the economy and war and peace.

Analysis of the Reagan–Mondale vote, made possible by television news exit polls, indicated the same sort of patterns. Despite the obvious religious differences between the parties, dramatized at the 1984 conventions by Governor Cuomo's speech in San Francisco and the role of Reverend Falwell in Dallas, Roman Catholics, according to CBS News, favored Reagan over Mondale by 58 to 41 percent. That figure just about matched the national margin, although Catholics did not vote Republican as heavily as white Protestants, who gave more than 75 percent of their votes to Reagan.

The only religiously identified groups which favored Mondale were Jews, who voted Democratic nationally by about two to one, and black Protestants, who voted Democratic by better than nine to one. To repeat a critical (and depressing) point: the American consensus that emerged in the 1984 election was, for all political purposes, a consensus of white America. Black Americans in 1984, as often in the past, were no part of the majority that ruled. In some states of the South, the most Protestant area of the country, the voting was almost exclusively racial, with whites voting for Reagan and blacks voting for Mondale. In Mississippi, whites went for Reagan by almost nine to one, while blacks supported Mondale almost unanimously. The populism that Reagan tapped effectively in the South was a white populism—effectively antiblack, just as earlier waves of Southern populism became anti-Negro by the late nineteenth century.

But Reagan only rode currents that were already running. Majority commitment to programs that were seen to favor only poor blacks—like affirmative action—had dissipated in national polls long before the 1980 election.

"I think white Americans have reached a consensus on black America," said John Seigenthaler, editor and publisher of *The Tennessean* in Nashville, as we talked one evening before the 1980 election, before Reagan took office, before the Justice Department became, in the eyes of many blacks, not their defender but their adversary. The consensus, Seigenthaler said, amounted to: "Look, we've done enough for the bastards. If they can make it, fine. If they can't, that's their problem."

The tightening of the screws on blacks, on government, on the freer lifestyles that had been celebrated in the 1960s and 1970s, may have already pushed blacks out of the American mainstream by the end of the 1970s. Many blacks may have agreed with the elements of the new consensus, but they had no active part in shaping it or making it. Black votes were not needed to become President, and black power was not needed to run the country. Reagan sensed that in 1980, and blacks were never a part of any Republican campaign calculations then or in 1984.

The Republican President may not have been antiblack, possibly didn't have any hostility at all toward people of color, but to him, those people were simply none of government's business and none of his business of politics. He made it clear, praising states' rights in Mississippi in 1980, that he wanted such things to keep going the way they were in the late '70s— and a lot farther back than that, too. When Reagan talked of civil rights, a rare thing for him, and of governing and the role of government, he sometimes seemed to be describing America in the late 1920s. He seemed nostalgic for a time and a life— hanging Calvin Coolidge's portrait in his office—that many Americans, black and white, never wanted to go back to. Franklin Roosevelt's revolutionary New Deal and its welfare-state concepts were in the foundation of national consensus. Ronald Reagan spent a lifetime trying to change that and could not. Being elected President was not enough. The people governed and they reminded him again of their commitment to New Deal attitudes on Election Day—rejecting his choices for Congress. That message from America was already understood by younger conservatives. "We are not here to repeal the New Deal," said one of the most conservative of the Republicans, the former Democrat, Senator Phil Gramm of Texas. "Our agenda is not to cut government, it is to contain the growth of government in the belief that the private sector, the national economy, will grow over it as time goes on."

On the other side, the Democratic Governor of Florida, Bob Graham, saw the immediate future of domestic politics this way: "There is some real sorting out going on right now. If it were linear, I'd say the Republicans are at 3 and we're at 7. We're both moving as fast as we can, and whoever gets to 5 first controls the United States for a long time."

So, the campaign that both candidates defiantly announced as a great ideological struggle, a choice between two visions of America, had in fact evolved into one fading vision of a more traditional America, Reagan's, and one uncertain critique, Mondale's.

"There is no real evidence that Reagan changed America ideologically," said William Schneider, a poll analyst at the American Enterprise Institute. "Polls don't show basic changes on questions like the role of government. All Reagan did in four years was change the agenda, what issues people were looking at, but those people were still skeptical that his ideas will work in the long run."

One of the polltakers studied by the institute, Daniel Yanke-lovich, put it this way:

> If you see the Reagan elections as part of a reaction to the sins of liberalism, then you expect a sorting-out process that will produce something different from either the old liberalism or the new conservatism. The set of values represented by the Reagan Administration policies—everything for the military, not a penny for education—is a momentary phase. Within a reasonable time, we will see a much more centrist and balanced position.

In other words, the Reagan years represented not so much a triumph of conservatism, new or old, or of the Republican Party, as they did a period of political redefinition establishing the assumptions and presumptions of postindustrial, post–New Deal, post–old liberal American politics. Ronald Reagan might one day be judged as a successful president and failed ideologue.

Americans in 1984, it seemed, agreed much more than they disagreed about the role and the size of their government at home and abroad.

The combined cost of domestic welfare and assertive influence almost everywhere in the world was going to be one-fifth to one-quarter of the wealth produced each year by the labor and machinery of the nation. The next public debates would not be over values or goals but about process. For at least four years (and almost certainly more) there would be debates and debacles in Washington about the methods of taxation to pay the costs of being a welfare-state superpower—by early 1985 Reagan was among those advocating "reform" of the income-tax structure, while others promoted such new revenue sources as national sales taxes or import surcharges—but the heart of the struggle was over whether the percentage of the gross national product going to the Federal Government would stabilize at 20 or 25 percent. The figure, for better or worse, was likely to be higher rather than lower, because of the way the majority chose to define themselves in 1984. Ronald Reagan could very well be remembered as a President who promised lower taxes for five or six years and then raised old ones and put in new ones to meet national demands for security at home and abroad.

But then, there is something in the dynamic of modern American democracy that pushes Presidents to routinely do and say the opposite of what they said and did as candidates or lesser officials. The man in the White House sometimes has to betray his old core constituency to serve an expanded consensus—usually because he is the only one who can contain the opposition of his old friends by convincing them of the inevitability of change. Reagan, if he found himself selling new taxes (and arms agreements with the Soviets), would be governing in the tradition of Jimmy Carter, who initiated American rearmament in the late 1970s after campaigning against increased defense spending, and of Richard Nixon, who reached out to Communist China after decades of condemning it as an evil empire.

Any president must inevitably become the chief executor of national consensus, with some being remembered for expanding the consensus even as it dictated to them. And Reagan would be remembered, even if his America, the consensus of his time, was different than the one he envisioned and pro-

100

moted for most of his public life. He made differences. If he had to become the defender of Social Security, the preserver of the welfare state—perhaps a more cost-effective one—he was able to bend millions of Americans to his will and conviction on many virtues of capitalism and the international role of superpower America.

Although he was forced to adopt the rhetoric of arms control, very possibly the reality of it, too, Reagan succeeded in striking the American "last best hope" chord to persuade many of his countrymen to pick up the messy baggage of Western colonialism around the world. He made Americans think again that the post-colonial world was an American world—or that they had to tote "the white man's burden"—and that effort left his opponents (including Mondale) little room to maneuver without endorsing military maneuvers. One commentator, William Pfaff of *The International Herald Tribune,* concluded that by the end of the 1984 campaign neither candidate "seemed prepared to accept the possibility that a sparrow might somewhere, sometime fall to the ground without this prompting an intervention by the U.S. embassy."

Two months later, in his second Inaugural Address, Reagan was saying, "God is the author of our song . . . [We are] called upon now to pass that dream onto a waiting and hopeful world."

An old song. Manifest Destiny. "We are a country manifestly called by the Almighty to a destiny that Greece and Rome in the days of their pride might have envied," said another President, Andrew Jackson, in 1824. The price of American pride had increased in 160 years as the country saw farther horizons, but the public's will (and its willingness to pay) had stiffened as the Carter years ended and the Reagan years began—and memories of sad destiny in Vietnam faded a bit more.

At that second Inaugural, President Reagan repeated his new commitment to arms control—certainly this time the public had done the governing—and, in fact, members of his Cabinet had already met with Soviet ministers to begin the tedious process of negotiating over how the negotiating would

101

be done. "Peace through strength" was a Reagan slogan, a brilliant one reinforcing popular pride in the United States's dominant world role while also touching dual insecurities of most Americans—fear of nuclear confrontation and uncertainty about Soviet military power and intentions. "Strength" did not seem debatable in the early 1980s. The range of dialogue went from arguments for massive buildup and new systems in space to a "freeze" at current levels of nuclear weaponry. The arguments were only over how much was enough. There was consensus on the strategy of deterrence, of strength. Reagan, though, inadvertently, created the "Peace" consensus himself, being forced to emphasize the word after national polling showed widespread fear that his bellicosity toward the Soviets might lead to nuclear war. Whatever his motivation, Reagan found his own new rhetoric as plausible as any other American. "There is a lure," the British weekly *The Economist* said at the end of 1984, "of going down in the history books as the man who first restored America's strength and then used that restored strength to strike a deal with the Russians." Reagan the Strong, even as he advocated more and new weapons, had to deliver "peace" if his rhetoric was to mean anything—and he had discovered that arms control was seen by many as some sort of substitute for genuine peace.

So the President energetically and rather successfully worked to shape the national security consensus emerging in 1980, but the people were in charge four years later on arms control. He was less successful both times in shaping policy or even finding effective policies in international economic matters. While many Americans enjoyed a "Reagan boom" at home— prosperity the President attributed to "free market" theory and some economists attributed to deficit spending—the United States position in international trade deteriorated disastrously. America's annual trade deficit was approaching $150 billion by 1985. Since "free market" and "free trade" were policies (or the lack of policy) that even the most powerful of nations could not easily impose on others, American demands for "industrial policy" rose in proportion to the decline of profitable trade and the jobs it produces at home.

The Politics of Individualism

To the ideological Reagan, the phrase itself, "industrial policy," was anathema, the ultimate government evil: interference in the marketplace. But it was a phrase likely to attach itself to the Reagan Presidency. The man in the White House was being surrounded by a consensus that something had to be done—something big, by government—to make American products more competitive in the world or to keep foreign products out of America. In fact, without uttering sweeping phrases, the Reagan Administration had begun experimenting with elements of industrial policy from industry incentives to "voluntary" import quotas on steel and other industrial products manufactured abroad. But that was not enough for many people, including the kind of men listened to in the Reagan White House. "We must change our approach to industrial life in this country," said Raymond Hay, chairman of LTV Corporation. "If that is formal or informal industrial policy, so be it." At the end of 1984, Kevin P. Phillips, one of the most influential of Republican thinkers, published a book with the title *Staying on Top: The Business Case for a National Industrial Strategy*.

They would be pushing Reagan. He was right that here the people govern—which can make it inconvenient for a president. But people don't think about presidents first, they think about themselves. They govern by acting as individuals. That is the way they vote, too. "They vote their pocketbooks."

And they did on November 6, 1984. In late September, the *Washington Post*/ABC News Poll questioned 1,507 registered voters across the country and found almost exact correlation between answers to the question of whether a person planned to vote for Reagan or Mondale and this question: "Under which one, Reagan or Mondale, do you think you will personally be better off financially?" Fifty-six percent answered "Reagan," and 40 percent answered "Mondale." Then the questioners checked the Reagan and Mondale voters against their answers on other questions. Voters who thought that Reagan was "unfair" but that his policies helped their personal finances were for him by almost three to one. Voters who thought there was a greater possibility of nuclear war if Reagan was reelected but that their own finances would be helped were for the President by better than two to one. Voters who said their own political views "matched" Mondale's, but that they would be better off financially under Reagan, were for the President by better than four to one.

The data were released by the *Post* in a story by Barry Sussman, the newspaper's polling director, on September 30. He offered this analysis, which contradicted the same day's front-page stories speculating that voters would cast their ballots for Reagan because they "liked" the President:

> Many voters say they think that Mondale would be better than Reagan at reducing the threat of nuclear war, but that they personally would be better off financially under Reagan. How would those people vote, as of now? By 68–31 percent, they back Reagan.
>
> Many voters say they feel that Mondale, more than Reagan, would see to it that government programs are fair to all, but that they personally would be better off financially with Reagan as president. How would they vote? By 71 percent to 27 percent, they support Reagan.
>
> About one quarter of registered voters say they feel the nation's economy is getting worse instead of better. Most of them support Mondale. But the ones in that category who think they personally will be better off financially under Reagan back the president, 70 percent to 27 percent. It is their personal finances, not the nation's economy, that count most.

The moral of those figures was that being well liked takes you only so far in politics. Nice guys often finish last, as Reagan would have done if he had come up for reelection in 1982. Nasty guys often win overwhelmingly, as Lyndon Johnson did in 1964 and Richard Nixon did in 1972. Democracy is, and is supposed to be, the sum total of millions of individual self-interests. People voted their own self-interest (as they perceived it), and mass movement was the product of those millions of self-interests—a politics of individualism.

104

That voting of perceived self-interest—a self-interest informed by the ceaseless images and data called an information revolution—diminished the partisan implications of the Reagan landslide. It was not very likely that the results represented or would lead to a "realignment" of American politics, with Reagan's party, the Republicans, winning enough new members to become the majority party. The political struggle and debate in the late 1980s would more likely first be carried out within the parties themselves, and then, with each election, the struggle would be within individuals choosing, for that moment, to side with one or the other.

In fact, although the Republicans began 1985 with lively, sometimes angry debates on tax and budget policy, most political action should shift into the Democratic Party sometime in the near future—because there are more Democrats and because there were few Democratic icons left to turn to after Reagan's huge victory. The Republicans were in power, inevitably subject to the same hubris that convinced Democrats they had caught the pulse of democracy in the 1960s. Soon enough, they found themselves slapped down, mocked as the party of the "3A's—amnesty, abortion and acid." And soon enough at the end of the 1980s Republicans could find themselves contending with their own excesses and delusions, vulnerable as the party of the "anti-A's"—antiabortion, antiaccommodation, antianything.

As the Democrats of the middle 1960s seemed fated for self-destruction in the embrace of American counterculture, the Republicans of the middle 1980s clung to a fervent subculture of minority beliefs—and a nasty sense of superiority. As young conservatives came to take their power for granted, they began to talk in public the way they once did in the more private regions of their wilderness.

In April of 1985, Eileen Marie Gardner, a Heritage Foundation analyst, was appointed special assistant to the Secretary of Education, who praised the originality of her thinking. Among her most original thoughts, it turned out, was that handicapped people were responsible for their own disabilities. "They falsely assume that the lottery of life has penalized them

105

at random," she had written a year before for Heritage. "That is not so. Nothing comes to an individual that he has not, at some point in his development, summoned."

At about the same time, at a testimonial dinner for Faith Ryan Whittlesey, who was leaving the White House staff to become ambassador to Switzerland, Peter B. Gemma, Jr., the director of the National Pro-Life Political Action Committee, praised the guest of honor by saying: "She's advocated the right-to-life for every pre-born baby. She seems to favor, however, monitoring the newborns until they're age eighteen, getting a voting analysis on them and then deciding who will be a productive member of society."

Gemma meant it as a joke. Among those laughing were the Reverend Falwell, Senator Jesse Helms of North Carolina and William Casey, the director of the Central Intelligence Agency. They were telling jokes like that around the Reagan White House.

Taste aside, there had to be eventual political trouble with "traditionalist" social issues like antiabortion. While they had helped Reagan and other Republicans (including Senator Helms) mobilize fervent constituencies, they were in fact opposed by the majority of voters. They are outside the new consensus and could one day drive away large numbers of voters, including those counted in the demographic discovery of 1984, "young, upwardly mobile professionals." The polls showed that these people felt comfortable supporting either a liberal Democrat (Gary Hart) or a conservative Republican (Ronald Reagan). That seeming contradiction made it startlingly clear that something more complicated than party realignment might be happening. Everett Carll Ladd, director of the Roper Center for Public Opinion Research at the University of Connecticut, was one of those who concluded that explanations for such things were more personal than partisan: "Contemporary political conflict is not so much between social groups, where politicians must bring together enough groups to establish a majority, as it is within individuals, where they must appeal to contrasting predispositions in the very same people."

Ladd was commenting on a series of national surveys on the

106

issue that fundamentally divided the campaigning and the rhetoric of 1984: the role of government. Do Americans agree, the surveys asked, with Mr. Reagan that "government is not the solution to our problems; government is the problem"? No and yes, according to the Roper surveys. "Almost no one 'out there' believes that," Dr. Ladd said.

> Most people have been led by their practical experience to view government as a persisting mix of the helpful and harmful.
>
> That a mass public would be at once strongly committed to expansive government and deeply troubled by it is important and new. So is the public's simultaneous commitment to extending individual choice (on social issues like abortion) and sensitivity to the negative consequences accruing from the exercise of this choice.
>
> The current mix of attitudes is as sweeping as those that have introduced new political eras in the past.

CHAPTER X

NEW CONSENSUS, NEW DEBATES

America works.

The land of the free delivers on its promises for most of the people most of the time. That fact has been central to my own understanding of American politics since at least 1972. In that year, Richard Nixon and George McGovern were the candidates for President. I passed through the neighborhood where I grew up, in Jersey City, New Jersey. The people living on Summit Avenue and Orchard Street, near the Jersey City Medical Center, in the 1950s were mostly Italians. The men worked with their hands, or their backs. The women stayed home and many of them still spoke Italian there. "College," "travel," "vacations"—those were only words, things for other people. A day at the Jersey shore was about the most anyone thought of in July or August.

They were Democrats, all of them, as far as I could tell.

Twenty years later, the people on Summit and Orchard were still Democrats—Protestants were Republicans!—but many others things had changed. There were cars around, new ones. Boats—people had boats in driveways and little yards. And their children, my friends, were gone—to the suburbs, to New York, to California. Many had become, as we used to say, "professional people." Dentists even, with big homes overlooking the water. Lawyers. A nurse, the wife of a big doctor in Morris County. A professor. The grandchildren of the people on Orchard Street were named Melissa and Jonathan and Lee.

That year, George McGovern, the candidate of their party, the Democrat, came along and said America didn't work. They thought he was crazy.

McGovern lost, even in Jersey City. The same thing happened to Barry Goldwater and Jimmy Carter, who tried to explain why they thought America wasn't working—and it happened to Walter Mondale in 1984. There doesn't seem to be much of a future in telling Americans that the country they built doesn't work. America does work—the real per-capita income of each American has tripled since I left Summit Avenue—and that fact may mean trouble down the road for some of the most energetic of the young politicians of the 1980s. Newt Gingrich's visions of the decline of Western civilization and Richard Lamm's sense that the American experiment is failing may have effective political half-lives of about ten years. American belief, optimism and common sense weren't invented by Ronald Reagan, but they served him well as they have others who would lead their fellow Americans in the pursuit of happiness.

Reagan rhetorically separated "America" and "government," reaffirming his faith in the one while attacking the other for holding it back. Fundamentally, the President saw America through the prism of individual experience: he was a poor boy made good. Jimmy Carter made a great political mistake in memorizing oil-consumption statistics rather than remembering his own rise from the red clay of Georgia to the White House.

For Reagan, for Carter, for millions of individuals, America worked—with happiness generally defined in economic terms. Politically, the system worked as well. The experiment of American democracy had succeeded, with great movements in the society governed by laws that seemed almost physical: in a free society, each action generated balancing reactions. Reaganism, then, began as an equal and opposite reaction to the forced higher taxation and forceful controls of the American welfare state, and the opposing forces reached a balance in 1984.

There were many political questions to be answered and disputes to be settled as the 1980s reached their midpoint, but there was a sense of national consensus on many, small and large. The pressure for reform of the Federal tax system was coming from both conservatives, led by Representative Jack Kemp, and liberals, led by Senator Bill Bradley. That was interesting enough, but what was remarkable was that both sides seemed to want the same reforms for the same reasons. Neither was advocating reduced overall revenues—a Reagan formula for reducing government's role; both argued that money lost because of lower rates would be made up for by closing loopholes.

"I've believed for a long time that the key to prosperity is a new tax system with lower rates and fewer loopholes," said Bradley. "There's a wide perception out there that the system is unfair. . . . The country's ripe for fundamental reform."

"I couldn't have said it better myself," said Kemp, who was sitting next to him at the time. "I take a little flak from some conservatives or libertarian people who don't think that we want more revenue. There are important things for the Government to be doing, from defending the country to many socially or economically desirable goals."

The same sort of coming together, of coming full circle ideologically, showed itself after the election when liberals again raised the issue of American aid and involvement in South Africa. President Reagan and most conservatives responded with time-tested evasions, saying that they were appalled by the South African Government's racial policies (apartheid) but were working quietly to persuade the country's leaders to

110

change their old ways. But thirty-five House Republicans, including many conservatives like Newt Gingrich, weren't quiet. They denounced the South African Government and demanded an American "sense of urgency" about apartheid.

Why? Gingrich and others said opposition to legal and open racialism was solidly within the American consensus and they wanted in, too. "The country's racial-policy debate is over," said one of the thirty-five, Representative Vin Weber of Minnesota. "It's time to move on."

There was also a sense of *that's settled, let's move on* in the actions and attitudes of many younger liberals anxious to separate themselves from the politics and power of organized labor. Like the New Deal, unions had done their job—Thank you! But the social welfare of the New Deal became permanent with almost every American a dues-paying member, eligible for benefits, while unions represented fewer and fewer Americans as the work and workplaces of America changed. Fewer men were necessary to mine coal, make steel, run railroads. Union membership dropped from more than 40 percent of the work force to less than 20 percent. The industries of the fifties were not the industries of the eighties, and "the solutions of the thirties were not the solutions of the eighties." Gary Hart and other new liberals who chanted that were just repeating the sounds of new consensus.

Certainly organized labor, as represented by its leadership, was not the solution to the 1980s political problems of Walter Mondale and his party. In fact, public attitudes about the role of labor transcended political organizing and debate—and predated political reactions by years. What happens in politics, in fact, has almost always already happened in the everyday life, the shared experience of Americans. The political consensus that became evident during the Presidential campaign only reflected a larger American consensus of shared assumptions, attitudes and aspirations—and Reagan's great success in 1984 (and 1980) was not so much in changing minds as in striking responsive chords. While Democrats talked of protecting industries, jobs and benefits, the members of unions like the United Auto Workers and the United Mine Workers were already accepting diminished contracts that no employers would have dared to seriously offer only a few years ago.

Many Americans, including many younger politicians and more than a few union members, seemed to believe that even the maintenance of existing labor standards and benefits was detrimental to American competitiveness around the world. The code word for unions among younger Democratic leaders was "old constituencies." This is the way it was used by Randall Rothenberg, author of the book *The Neoliberals*—"While old liberals continue to minister to old industries and old constituencies. . . ." And the leadership of labor really was old. There was no next career step for union leaders, and, once in place, they tended to stay there for decade after decade. They lost touch; they lost members. By 1984, there were fewer than 14 million left and that number was declining, too. The membership of the United Steel Workers of America dropped from 450,000 to less than 250,000 in just seven years, between 1977 and 1984. Politically, steelworkers and other union members were barely a "constituency." Solidarity, in American labor, was not forever. If organization made industrial workers a powerful constituency for more than three decades, it also made them middle-class. Most of them were the people and the families behind the statistics showing a tripling of American per-capita income. They had boats in the driveways, split-level homes, children in college and "middle-class concerns." More and more they voted their own concerns, voting as individuals.

The leaders of organized labor, some of whom were also leaders of the Democratic Party, were caught in a spiral of decline, and political activism was really a last resort. By 1984 they were reduced to hoping desperately that new laws, principally protective tariffs, and a friendly Democratic administration could somehow restore their position. But it was too late. Americans, non-union and union, reacted as a nation in the 1980s, perceiving themselves to be in a struggle to maintain world supremacy—economically, politically and militarily. The nation had known the satisfaction and the material benefit of global domination in the 1950s, when the United

112

States had accounted for half the world's gross production—the comparable 1983 figure was one-quarter—and per-capita income then was four times that in Japan. We were better off in the 1980s, much better off, but relatively the U.S. had declined. More Americans could afford better cars, but the better cars were being made overseas. Their quality had a lot to do with the fact that Japanese automobile manufacturing cost out at about $11 per man-hour while members of the United Auto Workers were receiving a total of $22 an hour in wages and benefits.

So, Americans were buying Toyotas, and the Japanese standard of living was rising rapidly—partly at American expense. But such things came to politics late in the international-economics game. What the candidates said and did were their responses to a reality that had already changed slightly. Whatever Reagan and Mondale said, automobile companies and auto workers, management and labor, were already moving to do what they could to insure their survival: it was in September of the election year that General Motors and the United Auto Workers agreed on a three-year contract that, in effect, began the relative reduction of auto-worker pay.

America worked. The systems seemed flexible enough to change. That might involve trauma: men learning new skills, families moving back and forth across the country, and politicians, particularly Democrats, accepting a new American status quo. But Americans had always moved and changed jobs, and American politicians are nothing if not adaptable. The problem with many Democrats in 1984, particularly Walter Mondale, was that they had not looked away from the mirrors of campaigning to glimpse the reality of a changed status quo. When they finally did that, they would become again the party of change in a nation of change. Republicans would represent that status quo, and would have to defend disintegrating sections of it, and Democrats would begin winning national elections again.

In the nation of change, today's consensus becomes tomorrow's contention. The consensus at the beginning of the second Reagan Administration would provide the base for critical dis-

113

agreement during the rest of the decade. Americans had accepted their free-enterprise welfare state and assertive world commitment, which had led to the consideration of another wave of fundamental questions about the role of the government of the strongest country in the world.

WHO PAYS? If the basic size of the Federal Government (which eventually means the amount of federal taxes) had been determined for a time, and if President Reagan gave up claims of reducing the size of things—he was reduced to trying only to slow its rate of growth—the question became: Who would pay the 20 to 25 percent of the gross national product going to Washington each year?

Whatever the name of the overhaul that led to tax reform or even a new system, the key to it would be the method and the total taxation of the great middle class. Liberals and some genuinely populist conservatives would try to push as much of the tax burden as possible onto "the rich" and corporations without taking so much that there was not sufficient capital available to underwrite future economic expansion. Most conservatives would try to push as much as possible the other way, onto the middle class, trying to maximize investment capital while being careful that the squeeze was not so tight that the middle millions wouldn't have enough expendable income to pay for the products and services of multinational corporate America.

SHOULD WE PREPARE FOR A WORLD WAR? After World War II, the United States adopted a "two-and-a-half-war" (conventional weapons) defense strategy, trying to maintain the capability to simultaneously fight major wars in both Europe and Asia and a small war somewhere else. After Vietnam, that became a "one-and-a-half-war" strategy, under the assumption that a chastened American public would be reluctant to support "small" wars and that if the United States and the Soviet Union were fighting on two continents, the conflict would inevitably become nuclear and total—and men and tanks and ships would become irrelevant. Then, convinced of widespread Soviet aggression beneath the threshold of all-out

114

nuclear war, the Reagan Administration began trying to fund a "three-and-a-half-war" strategy—say, Europe, Southeast Asia, the Persian Gulf and Nicaragua.

That is, nonnuclear world war. And it was called just that by Secretary of Defense Caspar Weinberger, who testified before Congress, "Our long-term goal is to be able to meet the demands of worldwide war, including concurrent reinforcement of Europe, deployment of Southeast Asia and the Pacific, and support for other areas . . ."

CAN WE IMPOSE A PAX AMERICANA? President Reagan, the missionary of "this last best hope of mankind on earth," seemed ready to revive the rituals of Manifest Destiny, the idea that America will save the world whether the world wants to be saved or not. We have been chosen to do that by God, the President said in beginning his second term.

"Our nation is poised for greatness," he said that day in January of 1985, ignoring 212 pretty good years. But we were indeed poised, technologically ready to experiment with the idea of filling God's skies with an electronic defense against nuclear missiles. "Star Wars": an unproved idea that the United States could become even more militarily invulnerable than it was during the centuries in which the oceans truly protected it from the armies of Europe and Asia.

At the least, a successful Star Wars defense would, in the dreams of Reagan and Weinberger, return the world's strategic balance toward its state in the post–World War II period, when the United States (after the technological breakthrough of the atomic bomb) clearly dominated the world.

Will it work? Can we afford it? Could the Soviets match us? What would they do if they realized they could not?

ARE WE REALLY OUR BROTHERS' KEEPERS? Or, perhaps, who are our brothers? The debate over social-welfare programs for the poor—not Social Security and the middle-class medical programs that constitute most of the spending of the welfare state—will continue to focus partly on the question of the definition of "family."

Beginning with the question of whether or not the rest of us

115

are really responsible for poverty in America, especially pervasive multigenerational black poverty, the debate on the poor among us has been reshaped by conservative scholarship being used to contend that government aid simply makes such things worse by making poor people less independent, less likely to help the poor by not being one of them. The logical consequence of that argument would be that all the country can do is try to maintain a growing economy for most of the nation— some of the poor have to benefit—and then combine just enough social welfare and enough police power to maintain tolerable public safety from angry or criminal people of poverty.

As questions like those dominate daily debate in Reagan's second term—a debate conducted against a background of record Federal spending and deficits—Democrats may finally get beyond the patter of the nightly news to begin trying to create a new context of ideas and issues for the campaign debates of 1988 and the 1990s. They might focus on three areas: a redefining of "national interest" as part of a modern foreign policy for a modernizing world; a persuasive reaffirming of the best of old-fashioned populism; and some creative pioneering in the relationship between the work of each American and the productivity of the nation.

Foreign policy in general and arms control in particular are the glamour zone of national politics—and it seems that it may be the first intellectual combat zone in the struggle for America's political future. In 1984, generally liberal institutions began doing what the conservatives had done twenty years before: putting money into thinking about alternatives to conventional wisdom and policy. The difference, even if many important Democrats had trouble comprehending it at the beginning of 1984, was that conservatives had shifted the conventions of the national dialogue. "The roles are reversed," said Edwin Feulner, the president of the very conservative Heritage Foundation. "Now we're in the mainstream and we will suffer for that as the liberals did before us. The intellectual ferment has begun on the left now. The foundations in New York, like Carnegie, Ford, the Rockefeller Brothers, are be-

116

ginning to finance study on nuclear issues. On arms control. The freeze. It takes years for ideas to break out, but they will. In a few years, perhaps, we'll be struggling against those ideas."

Feulner might have named even more. In addition to the work of the Carnegie Corporation, the Ford Foundation and the Rockefeller Brothers Fund, foreign-policy research concentrating on nuclear-war prevention was also being financed by the Field Foundation in New York, the George Gund Foundation in Cleveland, the Buffet Foundation in Omaha, and the W. Alton Jones Foundation of Charlottesville, Virginia. In addition, Ford, Rockefeller and the Guggenheim Foundation are also financing research and analysis on the role and impact of the new "ideas industry" itself, focusing on the influence of Heritage and the American Enterprise Institute.

"Our passion is coming back," said Richard J. Barnet, a founder of the Institute for Policy Studies, an organization comfortable with its "left-wing" label. "The passion of the right was greater and they understood that ideas are an investment in the political future. Their ideas reinforced each other and they changed national perceptions. Now it's our turn."

"The aim here," said the president of Carnegie, Dr. David A. Hamburg, "is to increase substantially the capacity of the scientific and scholarly community to analyze international conflict and to illuminate policy choices that tend to reduce the likelihood of nuclear war. . . . [We] will look at possibilities for fundamental long-term change in the relationship between the United States and the Soviet Union. . . . [We] will try to engage the ablest and best informed minds in generating new options, and will work toward a broader public understanding of ways in which the risk of nuclear war can be diminished."

If foundations are willing to do some of the thinking for the Democratic Party and liberalism in general, Democrats also have to do some of the hard parts for themselves, not only thinking about reducing the likelihood of big wars but dealing with the greater likelihood of unwinnable small wars. The Republicans' militant and military brand of internationalism had a logic of its own that seemed almost certain to lead to a confrontation somewhere over real or imagined national interests, real or imagined threats to national security: someday tough guys have to put up or shut up. But if the Republicans seemed headed for trouble—because, historically, Americans support only small wars that are quick and winning wars—the Democrats have to develop a logic of their own about where and why Americans should use economic, diplomatic or military force. In politics, you can't beat somebody with nobody or something with nothing, and the conservative militants doing the talking in the 1980s did know something about what they were doing in getting tough with friends and adversaries. They were trying to pressure "them" to be like "us."

There is, though, a great flaw in that strategy of talking tough: Americans are not and have never been tough ideologically.

Liberals must look to history as conservative thinkers have done so effectively over the past twenty years. There may be something to be said for aspects of isolationism in American politics—it is the American instinct. Warnings about "entangling alliances" go back to George Washington and Thomas Jefferson, so it is no accident that their political descendants shrink from casual intervention. When in doubt, don't!—worse slogans could be drawn from United States history.

For better or worse, Americans have interpreted their self-perception as "the last, best hope of mankind" to mean not that mankind must and will become like us, but that most of mankind just isn't good enough to be American. When the French followed Americans in revolution, in 1789, there was much talk of establishing an American-style republic on the old soil. Gouverneur Morris, the American ambassador in Paris, reacted with contempt, writing home: "They want an American Constitution without realizing they have no Americans to uphold it."

It may stem from arrogance or ignorance, but there is a common sense in maintaining a certain distance from peoples and situations beyond comprehension, be they French revolutionaries or Shiite Muslims. Such common sense about the power and the threat of small nations would be a good starting point in developing a Democratic alternative to a foreign policy that begins with the assumption that every sparrow that falls from every tree is America's business.

"Common sense" was a phrase Reagan used with devastating effect in 1980 while describing some of the foolishness of "bureaucrats" and "Washington" in the process of selling his version of populism—the little guys getting back at big government. But, four years later, voters seemed to have no trouble distinguishing between the irrationality built into any giant organism and the necessity and desirability of its purposes. Big government has survived, and the Democrats should now have their chance to revive the older and much more legitimate old populism of the little guys against the big money. The tax-reform debates of the 1980s provide the perfect political opportunity for old-fashioned populism. The question of "Who pays?" could provide a second range of usable issues for Democrats changing the question to "Whose side are you on?"

Are you with the frustrated farmers and workingmen who shouted for "progressive" taxation back in the 1890s to make the rich and the banks and the corporations pay their share—a greater share for those getting bigger shares of the national wealth? Or are you with Ronald Reagan and his friends who consider almost any redistribution of wealth as the beginning of something like the Russian Revolution. (Reagan has often and erroneously traced the idea of the progressive income tax back to devious communism rather than to angry farmers in Omaha.)

His own anger at higher tax rates for higher earners was a factor in Reagan's entry into political life. In the 1964 television speech he gave for Barry Goldwater—the title was "A Time for Choosing"—the actor said:

> We need true tax reform that will at least make a start toward restoring for our children the American dream that wealth is denied to no one, that each individual has the right to fly as high as his strength and ability will take him. The economist Sumner Schlicter has said, "If a visitor from Mars looked

119

at our tax policy, he would conclude it had been designed by a Communist spy to make free enterprise
unworkable."

Have we the courage, and the will, to face up to
the immorality and discrimination of the progressive
surtax, to demand a return to traditional propor-
tionate taxation? Many decades ago the Scottish
economist John Ramsey McCulloch said, "The moment you abandon the cardinal principle of exacting
from all individuals the same proportion of their income or their property, you are at sea without a rud-
der or compass and there is no amount of injustice
or folly you may not commit.

McCulloch's cardinal principle has long since been abandoned in the United States—often to the benefit of the rich or
anyone who can take advantage of tax shelters and deductions
ranging from interest payments on credit cards to yachts for
business entertaining—and the questions of reform are questions of who wins and who loses in the process. Even Reagan,
as President Reagan in May of 1985, abandoned the principle
he once preached to lead (or join) a bipartisan, bi-ideological
coalition proposing a simpler but still progressive tax code to
replace the complex progressive system that had evolved over
his lifetime. Both conservatives and liberals had come to share
the idea that the old system was so incomprehensible that it
was becoming counterproductive as more and more citizens,
believing it unfair, took it upon themselves to rewrite tax
rules. Cheating—in comfortable conscience.

But underneath the bipartisan consensus around "reform"
was the old argument across the decades between the first
Populists and Ronald Reagan. And the Democrats, even those
younger Democrats who advocated simpler taxation and overall lowering of rates, were with the men of Omaha. Governor
Bruce Babbitt of Arizona, one of the neoliberal Democrats
sometimes derided as a "Me-too Republican," did not say "Me
too" when it came to Republican tax philosophy.

Speaking after the 1984 election on the tax side, Babbitt
said:

I think there is going to be a sharp battle over the following proposition: Should we have a progressive tax system in this country? Now, there will be inevitable, predictable measures to raise more revenue, but the fight will be whether or not we should have a progressive income tax. Jack Kemp and Newt Gingrich and some of the folks out on the right are very openly going to be saying we should repeal the concept of progressive taxation. The rest of us will be standing up and saying, "No, Teddy Roosevelt was right." There is a powerful, equitable and moral argument for those who earn more in a society as richly endowed as ours to pay proportionately more. Now, you can argue about how much larger that proportion should be, but the bedrock issue that is going to separate us is whether or not those who have been most blessed by their efforts, and by chance, in this society have a somewhat greater obligation to pay the feed bill for common defense and all of the other tasks of government in this society.

A little class warfare—called "Populism," of course—wouldn't hurt the Democrats. Who pays? You, or the boys at the country club? Reagan made it clear that he was concerned about those folks, his people. At a White House briefing on tax reform, a month after the election, the President interrupted Treasury Department officials as they listed tax deductions that might be eliminated, with this question: "What about the country-club dues?

"A small-business man can advertise (and deduct the expense)," said the President, pressing home his point. "But lawyers and doctors depend on the country club to get new business."

If you accept that reasoning, the question is not getting government off the backs of lawyers and doctors; the question is whether or not other taxpayers should subsidize lawyers and doctors. Should the Federal Government use its power to (presumably) help legal and medical professionals generate business over golf or tennis—on the theory that such economic activity will eventually benefit all Americans? That theory is central to Reaganism and other variations of conservatism. It also points up the fact that all government policy favors elites or creates new ones. Since populism is rooted in anti-elitism, American politics is often a question of identifying the other side's elites and knocking the hell out of them. The populist Reagan, in the recent tradition of George Wallace, picked an intellectual elite: social planners, well-meaning professors, bureaucrats. Populist Democrats have to use tax-reform debates as a starting point to caricature the best friends and beneficiaries of Reagan and Reaganism and to heighten populist perceptions (and resentments). Who gets away without paying taxes? Who gets the breaks? Whose kids get into the best colleges? Who gets the best jobs?

If "they" do, then "we" have the angry makings of some political movement. "Equality of *opportunity*," the argument used by modern conservatives to counter egalitarian movements—which they sometimes attack effectively with the words "quotas" or "equality of results"—has to be examined somewhere along the line to see whether that "opportunity" produces anything more than verbal cover for the maintaining of privilege. Does equal opportunity to get into the best schools, for instance, mean anything if the tuition is beyond the financial reach of all but the people who already run the country or control a disproportionate share of its wealth?

The answer to that question, in fact, revealed a great deal of what conservative control of government proved to be about during the Reagan years. First, because the people who do get admitted into the best schools really do end up running the country. Second, because the reduced government pressure for egalitarianism and reduced government financial assistance for poor and middle-class students did reduce their number at places like Harvard, Yale and Princeton.

It is worth talking about those three schools, three of the oldest in the country, because to an extraordinary degree their graduates are America's leaders and always have been, beginning with eight Harvard men who signed the Declaration of Independence in 1776. From 1789 to 1980 more than one-quarter of the United States's "high federal officials"—Cabinet members and Supreme Court justices, for example—have been graduates of those three universities. On the Cabinet level that proportion has been increasing, not decreasing, since World War II.*

The makeup of future American governments, it seems, can always be seen there on the playing fields of the Ivy League. The greatest victory any American privileged class can have is getting their sons and daughters onto those fields—which means keeping out other children. Among the most significant battles of the "Reagan Revolution" were the ones fought to cut Federal aid for college tuition and Federal pressure to admit minority students to universities. Eliminating "quotas" and "government waste" was rhetorical cover for holding off people of color and ordinary salary from sharing equally in opportunity. Reagan proposals (after the election) to eliminate government-subsidized student loans to all families earning more than $32,500 a year and capping loans at $4,000 each year to families making less meant that all but the richest Americans would have to choose between no college and a second-rate college for their children. In the marketplace of America, that opportunity to run America would be effectively shared mostly by the children whose families could afford tuition and board that was approaching $20,000 a year at the best schools.

Whether or not all such cutbacks were ever accepted by Congress, the aid and enforcement reductions of the first four Reagan years had already reduced a democratizing statistic that had steadily risen throughout America's history—the proportion of children entering colleges whose parents had never attended one. That group, of course, included the overwhelming majority of college freshmen from minority groups. So, what happened next was predictable. At Harvard alone, the percentage of blacks in freshman classes fell from 8.7 to 6.3 percent from 1980 to 1984—at a time when there was a dramatic increase in the scores of black students taking college

* Detailed statistics on the relationship between education and public position in the United States since 1776 have been compiled and analyzed by Harry Burch, Jr., of Rutgers University.

admissions examinations. What didn't increase was black family income—and income was becoming the new criterion for admission.

"Life is unfair," said a rich President who graduated from Harvard, a Democrat, John F. Kennedy. "Some are born rich, some are born poor . . ." But the rules after birth did not have to be unfair. The countering Democratic idea to such Republican notions and manipulation of "equal opportunity" had to be some sort of enforced fairness. And the way to win support for such ideas was to convince enough people that they were systematically being treated unfairly. Populism! Democrats had to show most Americans that it was in their interest to have government referees—"government interferences," Reagan would say—on the fields of American opportunities.

The New Deal was government interference in the marketplace—over conservative protests—interference in the relationship between individuals and the economic institutions and forces of the country in the 1930s. It created the Democratic party that dominated the American political dialogue for almost fifty years—partly because Republicans did not want to talk about those issues. The Grand Old Party became a minority party then because, as Senator Bill Bradley said when we talked in San Francisco, "They did not consider social welfare part of the governmental process."

The New Jersey Senator was one of the younger Democrats coming to the conclusion that the emergence of a range of "workplace/leisure" issues might provide a third area (after some redefining of "national interest" and "populism") in which his party would grow in the future at the expense of the Republicans. "We have to create a work force motivated and anxious to provide what the country needs, greater productivity," he said. "The Republicans will not consider that part of the political process, so they will leave the field open to us."

What field? asked one of the toughest-minded Republicans of Bradley's generation, Senator Phil Gramm of Texas. He and I were talking, later in the campaign year, about the de-

124

cline of American heavy manufacturing. He was not disturbed: "I have no doubt that with the right economic environment"—he meant as little government regulation and taxation as possible—"the United States will become the lead nation in the world's next great economic wave."

I asked Gramm what he thought would be the elements—the technologies and businesses—of that postindustrial wave. He didn't answer for a few moments. He acted as if that question had never entered his mind—and I'm not sure it ever had.

"I don't know," he said finally. "It's not government's role to get involved in industrial decisions. Our only role is to provide the proper environment to allow the private sector to react to whatever is happening in the world."

Any government involvement, he added after another moment of reflection, would be "different words for socialism." That is how Republicans talked during the productivity crisis of the 1930s. They wanted government to have nothing to do with such things; and when the American people demanded government action, Republicans were eliminated from government.

It is hard to believe that any future declines in the United States's relative international economic competitiveness (or perceived declines in American living standards) will not soon be accompanied by public demands for government to "do something." Whatever Phil Gramm thought, his President, Ronald Reagan, was popular precisely because people thought he was doing something and that it was working for most Americans. There might be great future and hidden costs in Reagan's perceived success—huge deficits in the Federal budget and the balance of trade with the rest of the world, and millions of "displaced workers"—but inflation had stabilized for a time at close to traditional levels, and most people had money in their pockets most of the time.

If that changed, politics would change. New issues would emerge involving both national and individual productivity and the distribution of work and the benefits of work in the society. As more workers and their families were "displaced," the conservatives' "Opportunity Society" might be quickly displaced, too. Perhaps it could be replaced by liberal visions of something like a "Talent Society."

Edmund G. (Jerry) Brown, the former Democratic Governor of California whose own political career faltered even as his approaches were adopted by neoliberals like Hart, commented after the 1984 election that to keep up with the rest of the world America would soon be looking for every man and woman it could get. As always, he sounded both vague and utopian, but that is the way of former California governors.

> We need a national strategy that would enable Americans to both enjoy high wages and compete with nations that combine 21st century technology and 19th century wages. We don't make the rules of global competition, but increasingly we must learn to live by them. That means our literacy, our skill and our work product must equal and surpass our international competitors'. In this effort, all Americans need to participate. In the future we won't have enough talent unless we affirmatively reach out to those left behind.

One of the differences between the Democratic heritage and the Republican tradition is the sense of obligation that produces phrases like "those left behind." If we're all in this together, then we, the family of America, will have a lot of relatives "left behind" over the coming years. After the severe 1981–82 recession (the Reagan recession which brought down the Carter inflation) and the milder recession of 1979, more than eleven million workers lost their jobs. Of those, more than five million were classified by the Bureau of Labor Statistics as "displaced"—skilled and experienced men and women whose jobs disappeared.

The bureau reported that 11.5 million workers above the age of nineteen lost their jobs between January 1979 and January 1984. Its report (published in December of 1984) focused on the 5.1 million of those workers who had held their jobs—equipment operators, fabricators and laborers were the most common job titles—for more than three years. Only 3.1 million of these people found new jobs, usually doing other things at substantially less pay. The rest, two million people, found nothing.

Such dislocations and new ones coming in postindustrial waves have enormous social and, then, political consequences. And they represent only one of the work and productivity problems of the 1980s and the '90s.

That's change. It is progress. Fewer people are needed to make the country and the world work. But more people get hurt, at first. Unionized workers were being swept away in this wave. They were concentrated in heavy industries that were dying in the United States—the work moving to countries with cheaper labor or being automated. Companies, many of them already multinational, moved across oceans or borders, or to regions of the country with nonunion laws and work forces. Some went into bankruptcy, reopening their doors the next day with everything the same except labor contracts and wages. Some workers, desperate for their jobs, decertified their unions under management pressure. The word "givebacks" entered the language, union givebacks. The system adjusted. America worked, but more Americans were working at different things, usually for less money.

Work in America was changing. New labor movements and new forms of labor and compensation seemed inevitable. As the big old unions disintegrated, and their protection of workers with them, their necessary functions would be replaced in some way as more and more employees (including middle managers) sought the relative security of organization or individual contracts or lawsuits. And what management didn't like, it would fight—equal and opposite reactions. Changing politics would not be far behind—reflecting what had already happened "out there." As the twentieth century ended, the winners and losers in American politics could be determined by how parties and candidates encouraged, discouraged, confronted or avoided workplace changes and demands.

127

Another late-century political test seemed to be coming over issues concerning old poverty and new production organisms. Demands for new productivity and concerns for the uselessness and danger of a seemingly permanent underclass in the American welfare state were independently moving thinkers and politicians from both the right and the left toward schemes to employ that underclass as a trained, disciplined and low-paid work force capable of competing with workers in poorer countries.

It would not take much imagination at all to forge a consensus around conservative calls for "enterprise zones" and the elimination of minimum-wage laws and new liberal interest in preschooling for poor children. That combination of ideas from right to left could produce something like a comprehensive (and controversial) natural effort to attempt to mold a generation or two or three of poor (usually black) children into a productive citizenry.

Such programs would obviously be significant extensions of government power, almost an extension into state parenting of the children of multigenerational welfare. They would also be a classic example of how ideas and research work their way into politics and then policy. The idea of "enterprise zones" in inner-city slums or underpopulated rural areas—places where government would provide incentives and services to industries employing the previously unemployable—has been promoted from the right, particularly by the Heritage Foundation. The 1984 Republican platform and most conservative politicians have endorsed it, including President Reagan. The idea of beginning education of poor children at the age of three or four—getting them out of their homes and into a more disciplined environment—took hold (not for the first time) among liberals in late 1984 after the publication of a study tracing the lives of 123 pupils for twenty years in Ypsilanti, Michigan, and reporting that those with preschool education stayed in school longer and were less likely to end up on welfare or in jail. Besides, the Ypsilanti study indicated that preschool was cost-effective: by age nineteen the early starters had cost government $3,000 per capita less than other poor young people in social and criminal-processing costs.*

Free markets, early education, tax reform, unstoppable weapons and invulnerable defenses—the ideas are never really new, but are always changing slightly as the times change. And more and more politicians are out there looking for the set of ideas that will set them apart, as Ronald Reagan was projected by the sustained intellectual effort of American conservatives. Individual candidates of both parties, bouncing around within the legally rigid constrictions of the two-party system, will emerge or survive by finding the mix of ideas to reach individual voters. The campaigning will be practically one-to-one because candidates will be trying to "appeal to contrasting predispositions in the very same people."

That last phrase was the one used by Everett Carll Ladd of the Roper Center in discussing voters who were strongly committed to expansive government but troubled by the way it worked, and who were also committed to expanding individual social choice but disturbed by the consequence of such personal freedom. In the rather simple act of voting—yes or no, this one or that—those contradictions increasingly produce partisan votes difficult to explain by the old rules. The very same people who voted for a Republican President by almost two to one voted equally for Republican and Democratic Federal legislators and overwhelmingly for Democratic state legislators and local officials.

And next time they could do the opposite. Much was made of the fact that men and women under the age of twenty-five voted for Reagan in as heavy proportions as their elders. That seemed surprising to a generation of commentators who reflexively think of Republicans as a musty bunch. "You make those kids seem more complicated than they were," said Senator Daniel Evans, a Republican from the state of Washington who was a college president before coming to Wash-

* The study, done by the High/Scope Educational Research Foundation of Ypsilanti, Michigan, was titled: "Changed Lives—The Effects of the Perry Preschool Program on Youths Through Age 19."

ington, the city. "They've only known two Presidents, Jimmy Carter and Reagan. One failed, one didn't. They voted for the one who didn't fail. They had no memory of other men, other times."

In that, the youngest voters probably typified the nation. Americans are hardly a history-obsessed people. They go with what works now. Those under-twenty-five voters and the next older generation, including the young, upwardly mobile professionals, represent a good chunk of the country's immediate political future. On the evidence of both groups' simultaneous attractions to both Reagan and Gary Hart, it would be pretty hard to argue that younger Americans (white Americans) have yet chosen political sides.

"An upbeat supply-side Republican who renounced the Moral Majority's views and seemed genuinely concerned about peace could attract the yuppies and lock them into the GOP column," said one very interested observer, David Boaz, vice-president of the Cato Institute, the libertarian think tank generating research and ideas in the cause of less government.

> But if neoliberal Democrats really moved toward a market-oriented economics . . . in combination with their liberalism on foreign policy and social issues, they could become the party of the yuppies. It may well be that the intellectual vacuum in the Democratic party will be more conducive to such a new approach than the Reagan-dominated Republican party. There are special interests in both parties, and America's political future may well be determined by whether the Democrats declare their independence from the AFL-CIO before the Republicans break free of the Moral Majority.

Both of those declarations of independence were surely coming, but so were many others. Many of the ties that bound America were unraveling. For better or worse, the promises and fears of democracy were both coming true. Americans were gaining more power as individuals to decide how they would be governed, and most of them were prosperous and proud enough to make those decisions within an idealistic and stable framework of shared experience and assumptions. But the institutions that shaped and tempered national thinking, including the Democratic and Republican parties, were becoming more and more irrelevant to individuals. After all, it's only politics. And its future in America will be as dynamic (or as unstable) as a nation of individuals choosing between ideas whose time has come.

ACKNOWLEDGMENTS

THIS book began as a series of articles for *The New York Times Magazine* on the 1984 Presidential campaign. I am indebted to a number of people at the magazine for their help and encouragement and professionalism in the planning and editing of those pieces, beginning with the editor, Ed Klein. The others I worked with there included Marty Arnold, Jerry Gold, Ken Emerson, Barbara Dubivsky and Mary Ann Patrick.

The book itself owes a great deal to the talents of my editor at Simon and Schuster, Alice Mayhew. My assistant, Sally Harvey, lent skill and patience to every page, beginning with research for the first *Times* article in the fall of 1983. Jane Stone planned most of my convention coverage. I am also grateful for the help of Henry Ferris and Ann Godoff at

Simon and Schuster, and of my agents, Lynn Nesbit and Amanda Urban.

The discussion of American beliefs in Chapter I follows lines laid down by Louis Hartz in his book *The Liberal Tradition in America,* published in 1951, and a discussion of those ideas by Everett C. Ladd in a paper presented by the American Enterprise Institute for Public Policy Research.

As always, this couldn't have been done without the patience, caring and counsel of my wife, Catherine O'Neill. And I owe something, too, to the youngest of our five children, Fiona O'Neill Reeves, who was born on December 20, 1984, while I was working on the book. Nothing concentrates the mind so wonderfully—or, at least, so early in the day—as the predawn feedings of the first months of life.

RICHARD REEVES
New York, New York
April 1985

INDEX

Abshire, David M., 31
AEI. *See* American Enterprise
    Institute for Public Policy
    Research
AFL-CIO, 46, 131. *See also* or-
    ganized labor
air traffic controller strike, 17-18
Alba, Richard, 96
Allen, Richard V., 32
"American Creed," the, 11-12
American Enterprise Institute for
    Public Policy Research, 29-
    30, 31, 69-70, 99, 117
  financing of, 24, 31-32
Anderson, John, 41
Andrews, Richard L., 67
Anti-Masonic Party, 50
arms control
  as campaign issue, 80-81, 84
  in Democratic platform, 47-48
  the future of, 116-17
  Reagan's position on, 101-2
apartheid, 110-11
Armstrong, William L., 67
automobile industry, 113

Babbitt, Bruce, 46, 120-21
Baker, Howard, 65, 67, 70, 73, 75
Baker, James A., III, 69
Barnet, Richard J., 117
Baroody, William J., Jr., 29, 30,
    31

Baroody, William J., Sr., 29
Berger, Peter L., 24
Big Money, The (Dos Passos),
    77
blacks
  American attitude toward, 97
  Reagan administration's policies
      toward, 17, 128
  Reagan's attitude toward, 98
Blaine, James G., 53
Boaz, David, 130
Bork, Robert, 29
Bradley, Bill, 59, 124
  and tax reform, 110
Brock, Bill, 32
Brookings, Robert L., 28
Brookings Institute, 28, 29
Brown, Edmund G. (Jerry), 126
Bryan, William Jennings, 34
Buffet Foundation, 117
Burch, Harry, Jr., 123n
Bureau of Labor Statistics, 126
Bush, George, 65, 67, 69

Caddell, Patrick, 42, 91
Calhoun, John C., 50
Cantril, Hadley, 21-22, 71
Carey, Merrick, 70-71
Carnegie Corporation, 116-17
Carter, Jimmy, 109
  defeat of, 94
  defense policy under, 82, 100

135

Index

Carter, Jimmy (*cont.*)
   inflation under, 126
   "malaise" speech of, 91-92
Casey, William, 106
Catholic-Protestant split in politics, 53, 54, 57, 97
CATO Institute, 31, 130
Celeste, Richard, 47, 49-50, 51, 59
Center for Social Demographic Analysis, 96
Center for Strategic and International Affairs, 31-32
Center on Religion and Society, 24
Central America, 84
Chase Manhattan Bank, 32
Cisneros, Henry, 51, 55, 59, 62
Civil War, 74-75
Clinton, Bill, 49-50, 59
Connally, John, 73
consensus. *See* national consensus
Conservative Caucus, 64
Conservative Digest, 68
conventions, origins of, 50. *See also* Democratic Party; Republican Party
Coors, Joseph, 24, 32
Croly, Herbert, 76
Cronkite, Walter, 73
Crow, Trammell, 76-77
CSIS. *See* Center for Strategic and International Affairs
Cuomo, Mario, 45, 49-50, 52, 97
   "family of America" as theme of, 44
   marriage of, 55

Davis, Edwina, 53, 60
Deaver, Michael, 88
Defense Department, 114-15
   Reagan's attitude toward, 17
deficit spending, 64, 65, 66, 85-86
   Reagan's attitude toward, 17
democracy, and the "American Creed," 11
Democracy in America (de Tocqueville), 11, 16

Democratic Party
   and arms control, 116-17
   and blacks, 54, 57, 97
   composition of, 38, 49-62
   convention of (1984), 49-62
   and defense policy, 116-18
   and education, 122-24
   and the election of 1980, 19-21
   and the election of 1984, 21, 40-48, 49-62
   "family" as theme of, 52
   foreign policy ideas of, 47-48, 59, 60
   future of, 14, 105, 116-18
   and "idea entrepreneurs," 27
   and immigrants, 51-56, 59, 61
   and Jews, 97
   "national community" theme of, 42-43, 43-44
   and organized labor, 57, 58, 112
   platform of (1984), 47-48
   and populism, 34, 116, 119, 121-22
   and religion, 53, 54, 57, 97
   and taxation, 120-22
   themes of, 42, 43
   and women, 59
deregulation, 29, 30-31
devil theory, 43
DiLorenzo, Thomas, 31
Dolan, John T. (Terry), 67, 68, 69, 73
   at the Republican convention, 64, 66, 67
   and the conservative wing of the Republican Party, 65, 71, 73
Donaldson, Sam, 88
DosPassos, John, 77
Dow Chemical, 31
Dukakis, Michael, 51-52, 61
Durkheim, Émile, 24

education, 122-24, 128-29
elections
   of 1964, 28-29
   of 1968, 34
   of 1984, 9, 40-48, 49-62, 93

Index

Emerging Republican Majority, The (Phillips), 34
enterprise zones, 128
equality, and the "American Creed," 11
Etzioni, Amatai, 28
Evans, Daniel, 129-30
Exxon, 31

Fahrenkopf, Frank J., Jr., 74
Falwell, Jerry, 68, 97, 106
family, Democratic *vs.* Republican concept of, 44-45
Federalist, The, 19
Ferraro, Geraldine, 47, 50, 59, 96
Feulner, Edwin J., Jr., 24, 30, 31, 116-17
Ficklin, Henry, 53, 60
Field Foundation, 117
Fletcher, Norman, 56-57, 60
Ford, Gerald R., 16
Ford Foundation, 116-17
Foreign Affairs, 82
Free, Lloyd A., 21-22, 71
Freedom, and the "American Creed," 11
Friedman, Alan, 96

Galston, William, 25, 40, 41
Gardner, Eileen Marie, 105-6
Gemma, Peter B., 106
General Electric Company, 23
General Motors, 113
George Gund Foundation, 117
George Mason University, 31
Georgetown University, 31
George Washington University, 28
Gingrich, Newt, 109
    and apartheid, 111
    and Howard Baker, 70
    and the Republican Party, 67-68, 72-73
    and the Republican platform, 65, 66
Giordano, Joseph, 55-56
Glazer, Nathan, 28
Glenn, John, 57, 87

Goldwater, Barry
    and the election of 1964, 14, 23, 29, 109, 119
    at the Republican convention (1984), 75
government
    American attitude toward, 12-13, 16, 18-19, 21-22, 81-83, 92, 99-100, 106-7, 114-16
    Democratic attitude toward, 37
    Reagan's attitude toward, 13, 15-16, 18, 22
    Republican attitude toward, 36, 37
Government-Mandated Price Increases (Weidenbaum), 29-30
Graham, Bob, 59, 98-99
Gramm, Phil, 77-78, 98, 124-25
Grant, Ulysses S., 75
"Great Society," the, 28, 81-82
Grenada invasion, 84
Gromyko, Andrei A., 84
Guggenheim Foundation, 117

Hamburg, David A., 117
Hamilton, Alexander, 19, 20
Harris Surveys, 22
Hart, Gary, 130
    blacklisted by USIA, 73
    and the Democratic Party, 52
    foreign policy ideas of, 48, 60
    Glazer's comments on, 28
    industrial strategy theme of, 45-46
    and *A New Democracy,* 45
    "new ideas" theme of, 25, 42
    1984 campaign of, 26-27, 58, 59, 95, 96
    and organized labor, 46, 111
    pragmatism theme of, 43, 46
    and television, 95, 96
Harvard University, 28, 122-24
Hatfield, Mark O., 67
Hay, Raymond, 103
Helms, Jesse, 106
Heritage Foundation, 116, 117
    activities of, 30-31
    and enterprise zones, 128

Index

Heritage Foundation (*cont.*)
  financing of, 24, 31-32
  and Eileen Marie Gardner,
    105-6
High/Scope Educational Research
  Foundation, 129*n*
Hoover, Herbert, 29
Hoover Institution, 29, 30
House Un-American Activities
  Committee, 35
Hunt, Nelson Bunker, 69
Hyland, William, 82

ideas
  kinds of, 26-27
  as a political force, 9, 14, 25,
    32
"ideas industry," the, 10, 23-32,
  116-17
immigrants, 51-56
  assimilation of, 55
  political identity of, 96
individualism, 18-19, 33-34
  and the "American Creed," 11
  political and social *vs.* eco-
    nomic, 13
industrial strategy, 28
  in Democratic campaign, 41-
    42, 45-46
  in Hart's campaign, 26-27
  Reagan's attitude toward, 102-
    103
Institute for Policy Studies, 117
internationalism, 20
isolationism, 20, 47-48
Italian Americans, 55-56, 96

Jackson, Andrew, 34, 50, 101
Jackson, Barry, 63, 68
Jackson, Jesse, 27, 50, 52, 59
  foreign policy ideas of, 42
Japan, 113
Jarvis, Howard, 85
Jefferson, Thomas, 19, 33-34, 35
Johnson, Lyndon, 14, 81, 104
Jones, Matthew, 58, 60
Jones, W. Alton, Foundation, 117
Justice Department, 17, 97

Kaplan, Martin, 43, 44, 45, 85,
  93-94
Kemp, Jack, 67, 70, 85
  and tax reform, 110
Kennedy, Edward M., 30, 50
Kennedy, John F., 124
Kennedy, Robert, 60
Kennedy School of Government,
  Harvard, 27
Keynes, John Maynard, 85-86
King, Coretta Scott, 73
Kirkpatrick, Jeane, 29
Kissinger, Henry, 32
Korean Airlines Flight 007, 30
Kristol, Irving, 25-26

labor. *See* organized labor
Ladd, Everett Carll, 106-7, 129
Laffer, Arthur, 27, 70, 85-86
Laffer Curve, 32
Laird, Melvin, 31
Lamm, Richard, 46, 49-50, 59,
  109
Lara, Elizabeth, 52, 53, 60
Lewis, Sinclair, 77
Lincoln, Abraham, 36
Lippmann, Walter, 42, 43
Lott, Trent, 67-68, 71
LTV Corporation, 103

McCarthy, Joseph, 35
McCulloch, John Ramsey, 120
McDonald, Carla, 52, 54, 58, 60-
  61
McGovern, George, 28, 60, 108,
  109
McKenzie, Shirley, 78
*MacNeil/Lehrer News Hour,
  The,* 90
Madison, James, 19, 20
*Main Currents in American
  Thought* (Parrington), 37
Mainstream Committee, Republi-
  can Party, 63, 68, 73
*Making of the President, 1960,
  The,* 86
Manifest Destiny, 101
Massachusetts Institute of
  Technology, 28

Index

Mathias, Charles McC., Jr.
  at the 1984 convention, 64, 68, 71
  and the conservative wing of the Republican Party, 66-67, 73
"Mediating Structures in Public Policy," 24
Medicare, 22
Michel, Robert H., 67
Mondale, Walter, 9, 27, 56
  campaign positions of, 37, 80-81, 82, 83, 84, 85
  and Carter's "malaise" speech, 91n
  and the debates, 26, 79-80, 85, 89-90
  defeat of, 9, 109
  foreign policy ideas of, 47-48
  "ideas retreats" of, 41
  New Deal politics of, 42, 51, 61
  and organized labor, 46
  political tactics of, 94-95, 95-96
  presidential campaign of, 40-48
  press coverage of, 87, 90
  "realism" theme of, 48
Moral Majority, the, 68, 131
Moynihan, Daniel Patrick, 32
"Myth of Government Job Creation, The," 31

National Black Republican Council, 78
National Committee for Survival of a Free Congress, 69
national consensus, 110
  blacks left out of, 97-98
  on foreign policy, 82, 84
  on organized labor, 111
  and polltaking, 81, 83-84
  on race, 111
  on role of government, 12-13, 81, 83, 92, 106-7
  on tradition, 85-86, 120
  on the welfare state, 81-82, 98
National Conservative Political Action Committee, 67, 69
neoliberals, 46, 50, 120-21

and the Democratic Party, 58-59
Neoliberals, The (Rothenberg), 112
Neuhaus, Richard John, 24
New Deal
  and the Democratic Party, 124
  and Mondale, 51, 61
  national consensus on, 81-82, 98
  and populism, 35
New Democracy, A (Hart), 45
New Republicans, 73
Newman, Dorothy, 58, 60
Next American Frontier, The (Reich), 27
NICPAC. See National Conservative Political Action Committee
Nisbet, Robert, 24
Nixon, Richard M., 16, 100, 104
Nofziger, Lyn, 69
Nunn, Sam, 59

O'Neill, Thomas P., 37
organized labor, 46, 111-13, 127
Ortega, Katherine, 63, 64

Palmer, John J., 91
"paradigms," 27
Parrington, Vernon, 37n
"partisan ideas," 26
Penner, Rudolph, 29
People's Party, 36
Pétain, Marshal, 25n
Pfaff, William, 101
Phillips, Howard, 64, 67, 68, 69
Phillips, Kevin P., 34, 103
Plesser, Tully, 81, 83
"policy ideas," 26, 27
Political Beliefs of Americans (Free and Cantril), 21-22
polls
  on foreign policy, 84-85
  and the campaign of 1984, 103-4
  on the role of government, 81-82, 99, 106-7
  techniques of, 83-84

Index

populism
  and the Democratic Party, 34-
    35, 116
  history of, 34, 35, 36
  and religion, 34, 35
  and the Republican Party, 34-
    37, 39
  Republican style of *vs.* Demo-
    cratic, 119, 122
  and taxation, 121-22
Populists, 34, 39
pres coverage of politics, 86-90
Price, David, 57, 61
Princeton University, 122-23
private property, 11
productivity, 113, 116, 125, 128
Progressives, 35
Proposition 13, 85
Protestants, political alignment of,
  53, 54, 57
Public Agenda Foundation, 84
Public Interest, The, 25-26, 28
puffery, 27

Reagan, Ronald
  and arms control, 80, 84,
    101-2
  attacks on government by, 13,
    15-16, 18, 22, 209
  balance of trade under, 102-3
  and blacks, 17, 97-98, 128
  campaign theme of (1980), 25
  career of, 10, 73
  and debates (1984), 79-80, 89-
    90
  defense policies of, 19-21, 82,
    101-2, 115, 117-18
  and the deficit, 17, 65, 66, 85-
    86
  education policy under, 122-24,
    128
  environmental policy of, 17
  foreign policy of, 101, 115
  Giordano anecdote told by, 55-
    56
  health of, 65
  Inaugural Address (1984), 101
  and industrial policy, 102-3
  labor policies of, 17-18

  leadership of, 19-20, 94
  1964 speech of, 35
  nomination of (1984), 63-64
  as nucleus of Republican Party,
    67-68, 74
  political strategy of, 19-20
  populism of, 10, 34-37, 39, 119,
    122
  press coverage of, 87-90
  and Social Security, 80, 101
  and South Africa, 110-11
  tax policies of, 17, 100, 114,
    119-20, 121-22
  and voters' self-interest, 104-5
  and the welfare state, 12-13, 22
  victory of (1984), 9, 93-94
Reagan Experiment, The, 91
Reaganism, 18
Reagan Record, The, 82, 91
"regime ideas," 26
Reich, Robert B., 26-27, 41-42,
  45, 48
Republican Mainstream Committee, 63, 68, 73
Republican National Committee,
  32, 83
Republican Party
  as "America's Party," 13-14,
    74
  and blacks, 53, 54, 111
  composition of, 38, 63-78
  Conservative Caucus of, 64
  convention of (1984), 63-78
  and deficit spending, 64, 65, 66
  exclusivity of, 72-73, 74
  and the "ideas industry," 23-24
  and immigrants, 53
  loyalty in, 73-74
  Mainstream Committee of, 63,
    68, 73
  moderates in, 63, 68, 71-72, 73
  "New Republicans" in, 73
  in the 1980 election, 19-21
  platform of (1980), 15-16, 17,
    24, 30
  platform of (1984), 65, 66
  and Protestants, 57
  and religion, 54, 57, 97
  and the welfare state, 71-72

140

Index

Resource Bank, 30-31
Rockefeller Brothers Fund, 116-117
Roman Catholics, political alignment of, 53, 54, 57
Roosevelt, Franklin, 34, 42, 43, 91-92, 98
Roper Center for Public Opinion Research, 106-7, 129
Roth, William, 85
Rothenberg, Randall, 112
rule of law, 11

Sawhill, Isabel V., 91
Scaife, Richard Mellon, 32
Schlichter, Sumner, 119
Schneider, William, 69-70, 99
Seigenthaler, John, 97
slogans, 26, 27
Social Security, 22, 80, 101. *See also* welfare state
South Africa, 110-11
Squier, Robert, 83-84
Stanford University, 29
"Star Wars," 115
Staying on Top (Phillips), 103
Stein, Herbert, 32
Stockman, David, 68, 83
"supply-side economics," 25, 27, 32, 70, 85
Sussman, Barry, 104

Taft, William Howard, 68
taxation, 17, 110, 114, 119-22
tax revolts, 85
television, political effect of, 95-96
Tennessean, The, 97
"testifiers," 30
Thurow, Lester C., 28, 45
Thurmond, Strom, 73
"To Empower People" (booklet), 24, 29

Tocqueville, Alexis de, 11, 16
TRW, 32

United Auto Workers, 111-12, 113
United Mine Workers, 111-12
United States Information Agency, 73
United Steel Workers of America, 112
Urban Institute, 82, 91

Van Buren, Martin, 50
Viguerie, Richard, 68-69, 70, 71

Wallace, George C., 34, 122
Warner, John, 69
Washington, George, 35
Watt, James, 32
Weber, Vin, 111
Weicker, Lowell P., Jr., 67, 68, 73
Weidenbaum, Murray, 29-30
Weinberger, Caspar, 115
welfare state, the, 91, 115-16
  cost of, 100
  national consensus on, 71-72, 81-82, 98
  Reagan's attacks on, 12-13, 83
Weyrich, Paul, 69
White, Theodore, 86-87
Whittlesey, Faith Ryan, 106
William of Ockham, 75
Wilson, James Q., 26, 27
Winthrop, John, 44

Yale University, 122-23
Yankelovich, Daniel, 84-85, 99
Ypsilanti Study of early education, 128-29
"yuppies," 58, 61

Zimmerman, Paul, 74

141

ABOUT THE AUTHOR

RICHARD REEVES is the author of six books, most recently *Passage to Peshawar* and *American Journey: Traveling with Tocqueville in Search of Democracy in America.* He is a syndicated columnist, published twice weekly in more than 150 newspapers, and writes regularly for *The New Yorker* and *The New York Times Magazine.* He has written and hosted seven network documentary films, winning all of television's major documentary honors, the Emmy (1980), the Columbia–Dupont Award (1984) and the George Foster Peabody Award (1984).